Drawing Bears : How to Draw Bears
For the Beginner

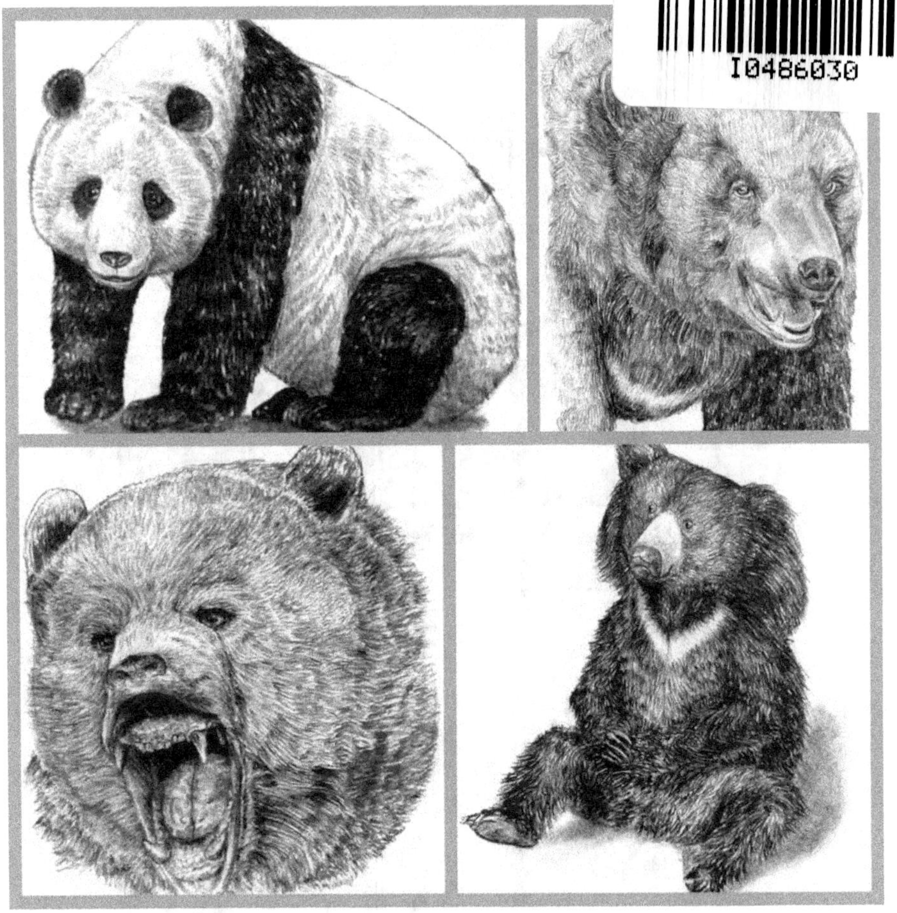

Learn to Draw Series
Adrian Sanqui

Mendon Cottage Books

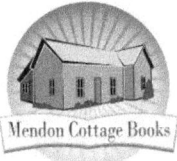

JD-Biz Publishing

Learn How to Draw Books for the Absolute Beginner

Table of Contents

Drawing tools 4

   Pencils 4

   Charcoal pencils 5

   Mechanical pencil 5

   Sharpener..6

   Erasers 6

   Smudge sticks...8

   Coloring materials 9

Common Gestures of a Bear 11

   Standing or walking on shoulder height................................11

   Standing on two legs 12

   Sitting 13

Sloth Bear 15

Giant Panda 23

Black Bear 33

Growling Bear 41

Author Bio...50

Publisher...56

Drawing tools

Pencils

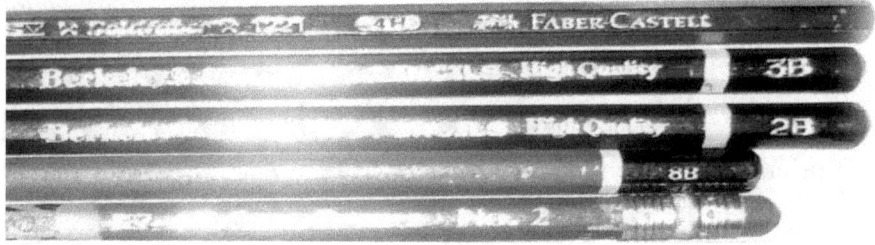

The most important tool you need to be able to enhance your drawing skills is a medium that can be corrected if you made some sloppy line strokes. Knowing and using more than just one type of pencil is a big help and it is better if you have pencils of different grades so you can easily produce the kind of lightness or darkness you want to make. The 'H' engraved near the pencil's tip (side of eraser) stands for "hardness" and it ranges from 2H to 9H. A pencil with only an "H" mark and doesn't have a number means 1H. The most common type (the one available anywhere) of pencil that does not indicate its grade mark is usually a 2H pencil. The "B" marking of pencils stand for "blackness", this means that they can easily produce darker line marks and are softer than H pencils. It ranges from HB (hard and dark) to 9B (very soft and very dark), so when it comes to B pencils, the higher the number is; the softer and darker it becomes. Different brands have different softness, hardness and blackness levels, so if you are going to use a certain brand for the first time, you should try them out first before applying it on your main drawing.

Charcoal pencils

Charcoal pencils also come in different grades. The generic grades of soft, medium and hard are available in different brands. Charcoal pencils are a bit messy to work with; even the 'hard' grade charcoal pencil is still relatively softer compared to those with 4B to 6B grade pencils. It is most advisable for drawings that would require a lot of smeared shading for a smoother and wider portrayal of gradation.

Mechanical pencil

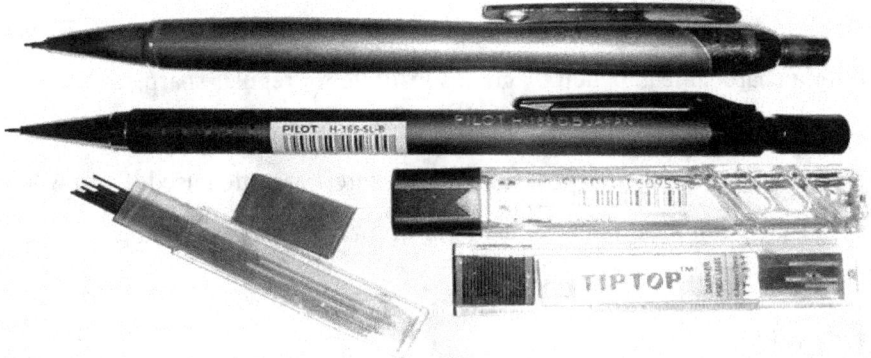

A mechanical pencil has a consistent wick or point which makes it easier for you to maintain the thickness of the line marks you produce. Mechanical pencils are good for small and subtle detailing that requires very thin lines, instead of sharpening your pencil several times just to have a thin and constant fine point that you need. Different grades of lead or graphite is also available for refilling your mechanical pencil, just make sure that the size of the point your pencil has is also the same as the pencil leads you refill it with. They come in several sizes and style, but what really matters is it does what it's supposed to.

Sharpener

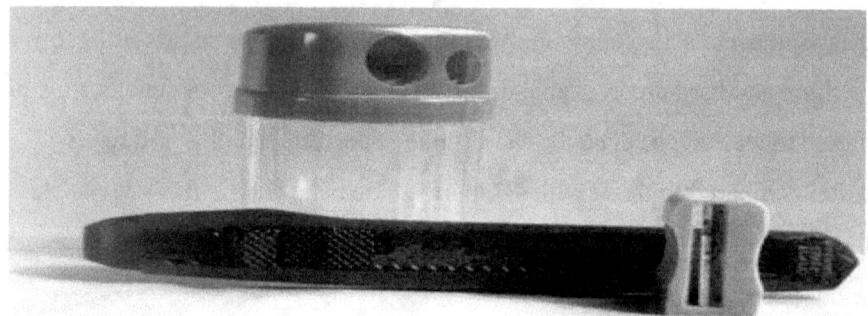

A regular sharpener is quite dependable if you are using H and low B pencils, but if you are going to use it to sharpen a pencil with very soft graphite cores then it may keep on breaking, most especially if you will use it for a charcoal lead pencil. A good substitute for regular sharpeners is a cutter, so you can easily control the pressure that should just be enough to expose the core and achieve a fine point. Cutters are often used if you want a "chisel" point pencil that is very helpful for thick and thin linings.

Erasers

Pencils are no good if you don't have a good quality eraser, having an eraser is essential if you are going to use a pencil for drawing. Choose a rubber eraser that is soft and not the ones that leave a faint color or worst is a scratch on the paper.

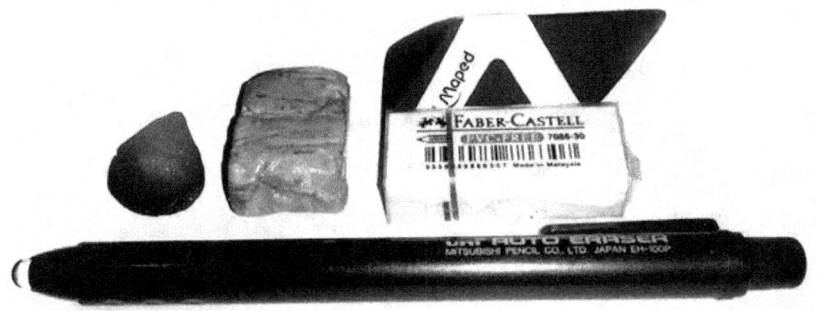

Don't leave your eraser lying around on the table or just anywhere, keep it on a pencil case or anything that can protect it from being exposed on air for too long because some erasers (cheaper ones) harden when it's left lying around because it will dry out and harden.

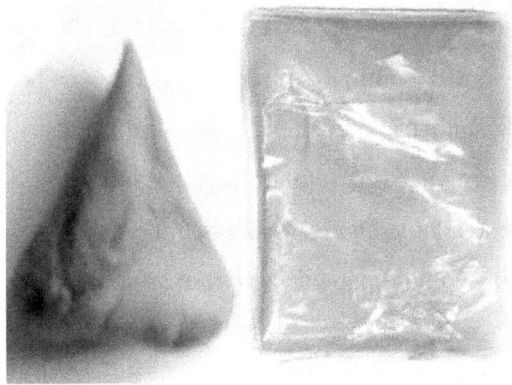

A kneadable eraser is very helpful for making highlights and reaching hardly accessible areas such as the gloss on the eyes or light portions of fingernails and such. It usually looks like a gray slab or a small bar of clay that can be molded or deformed to any shape you desire. It doesn't rub off the marking like usual erasers, but instead, it lifts off the graphite from the paper, like absorbing it. Instead of rubbing the eraser with a certain pressure to remove a marking, carefully dab on the portions you want to erase or to simply decrease the applied graphite or charcoal until you recover the brightness (whiteness of the paper) you want. Kneaded erasers can still be useful as long as they aren't already too dirty or dry. Keep it in a concealed container to lengthen its usefulness, because just like how good it is for absorbing graphite, it would also easily catch dust.

Smudge sticks

A smudge stick is used for smearing the shades on the portions that are hard to access. Some artists dull down the other tip so it can be used for distributing the shades on the big areas. To avoid ruining the smudge stick, use a sand paper to make a blunter tip or to make it even pointier. Smudge sticks or blending stumps comes in different sizes, choose what best fits your needs and it will be a big help for blending gradations. Smudge sticks are cheap and are available on art stores. Common smudge sticks are just rolled and compressed hard papers, so try not to get it wet.

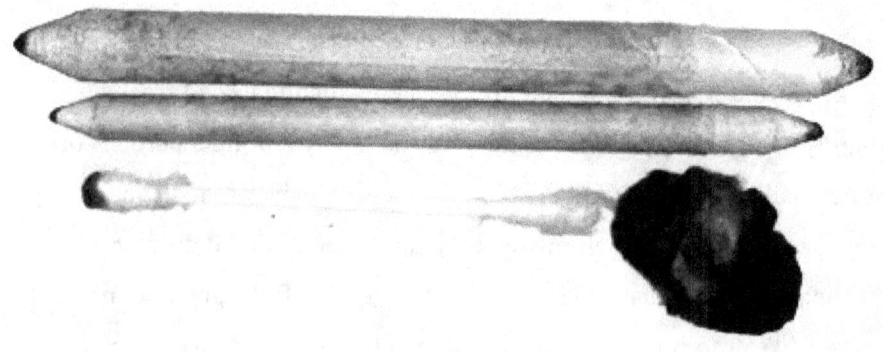

Keep those used up smudge sticks even if it's already in a rugged state (dirty or worn out), you never know when it might get handy. Dirty smudge sticks are useful for producing faint shades, and those with torn up tips can make textures that you might find useful.

If ever you cannot find a smudge stick available (although, I doubt this would be a problem if you have art stores near you, and if not, you can just order online. It is quite cheap) you can just make a tortillion for a temporary smudging tool (some artists actually prefer this one instead of smudge sticks). Use a thick piece of paper (like those on sketch pads, preferably the ones for watercolor drawings. Do not use thin and shiny papers). Fold it on one side and roll it up to create a cone, with the folded side at the tip.

Coloring materials

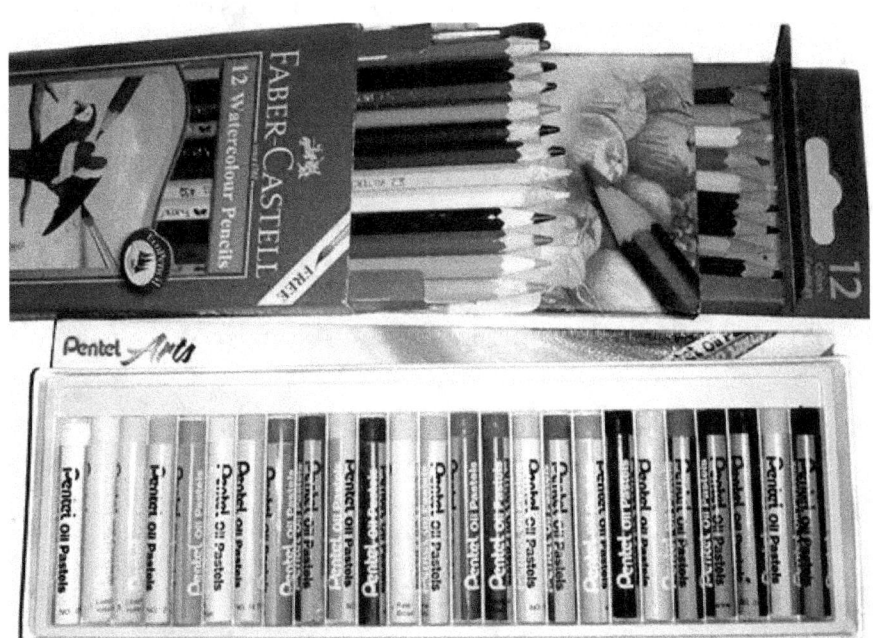

If you are planning to color your drawing, choose a coloring tool that best fits your needs.

Oil pastels are good for blending and synchronizing different colors together. It might get messy on your first trials (if you don't want to get messy, just place a clean piece of paper for your palm rest, to avoid rubbing your palm against the colored portions of your drawing) but you'll get the hang of it as you use it more often. Oil pastels are good for beginners as a practicing tool for smearing different color values.

Color pencils are the next best thing for filling your drawing with colored hatches (linear shading), or even coloring via scribbling. This coloring tool is best for small-sized illustrations. Although, the peak of the tone values that a common color pencil set can produce are far weaker than the oil pastel's, and it cannot be smeared (but there are available color pencils which can produce strong color tones just like oil pastel's or even acrylic's, but they are quite pricy; like the prisma color pencils). This coloring tool is also a good practicing medium for beginners, and my personal favorite for quick colored sketches or even for illustrations with fairly detailed line work.

Common Gestures of a Bear

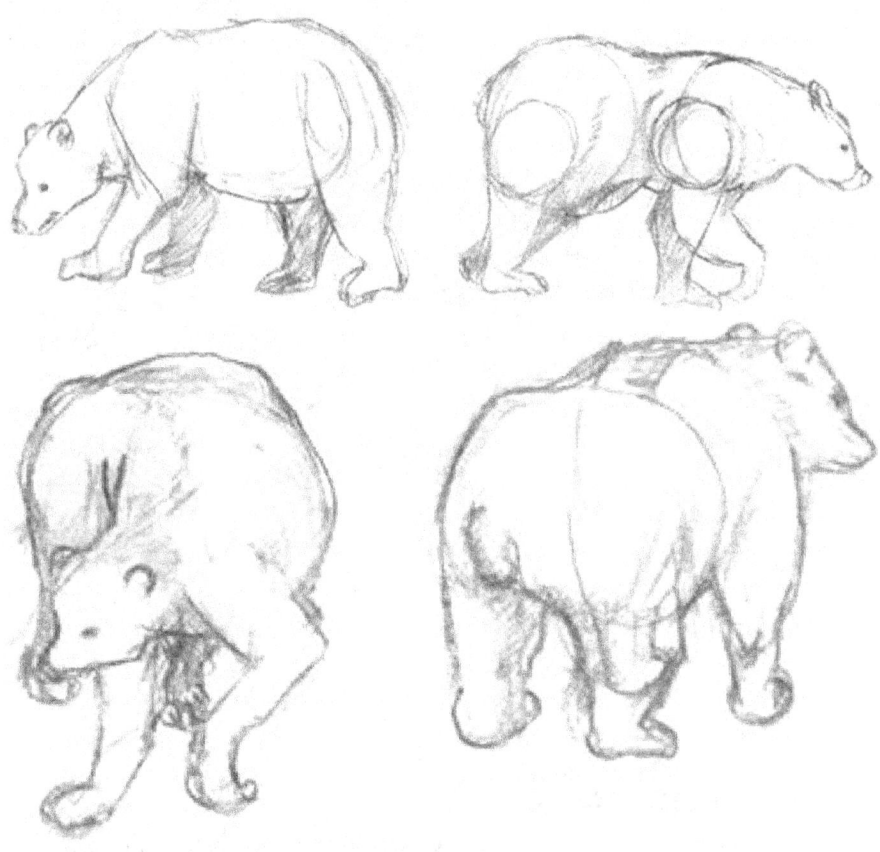

Standing or walking on shoulder height

Because they travel by walking with their four feet, bears are often seen standing on their shoulder's height. Some bears have thicker-looking hind legs because of thicker fur on their lower body. The forelegs of bears appear relatively longer compared to their hind legs (especially those who can climb trees) because their lower body has a rounder mass. The difference in leg length (distance from the base or body) is apparent on adult bears and but it is hardly observable when they are walking.

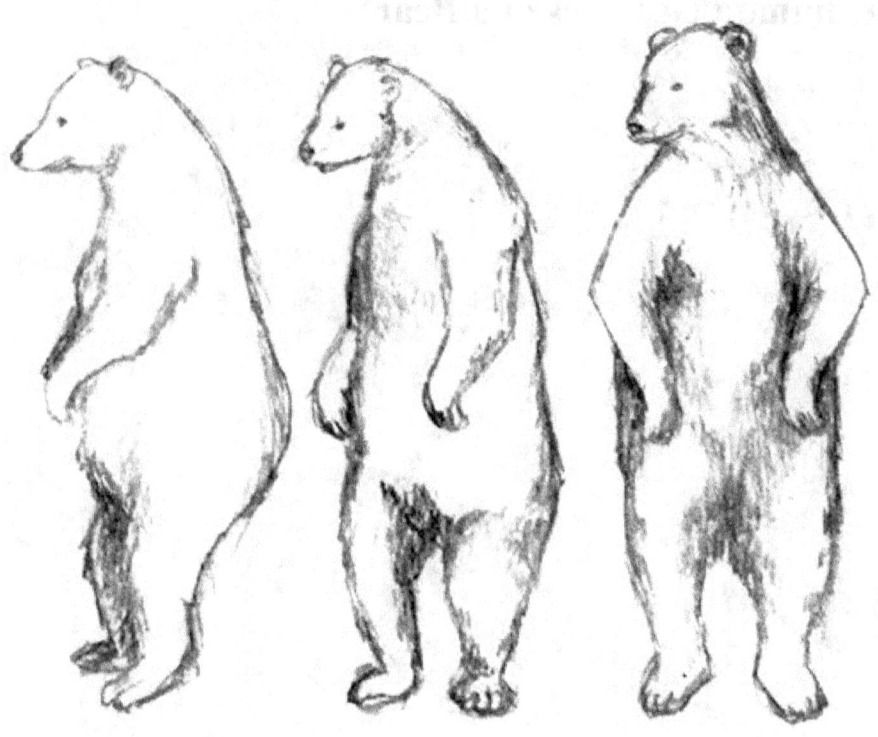

Standing on two legs

Bears stand on their hind legs when they are reaching for something (primarily, food). But most of the time they stand to display their size and intimidate; if they become defensive, disturbed, irritated or threatened.

Bears don't have dominant shoulder lines like humans, their shoulders are sloped downward because of their thick necks and big heads. When standing, bears are slightly slouching; with their arms (forelimbs) crooked forward and paws down. Their legs (back limbs) are short and always apart. Due to their thick fuzzy fur, they appear bigger than they already are.

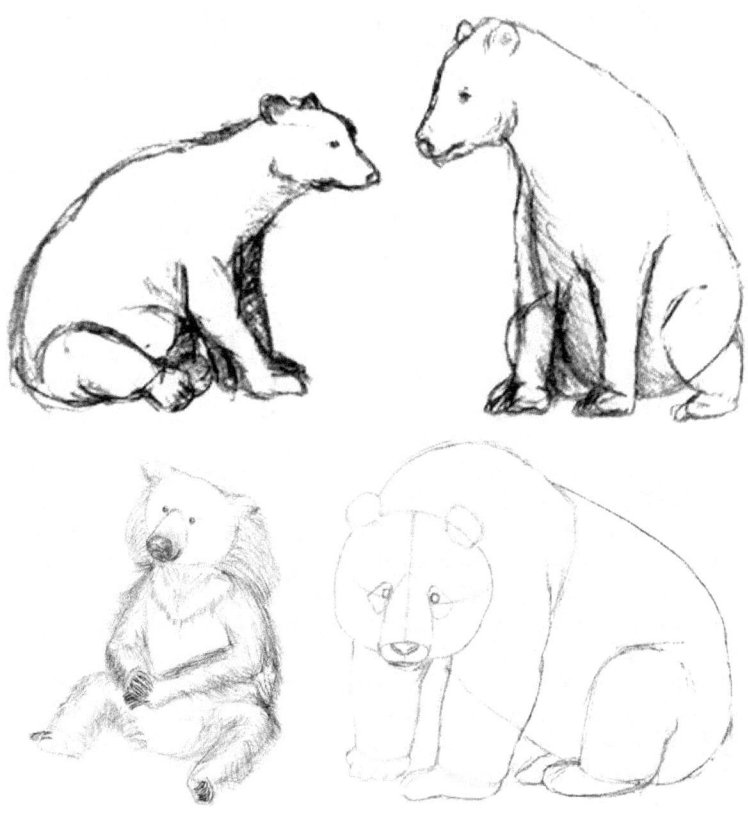

Sitting

Bears often sit in a squat position, with their hind legs folded and wide apart and their four paws touching the ground (like a sitting position of a cat or a dog). Because of their huge bodies, their short hind legs are always on the sides and wide apart when they sit. And to maintain balance (and so they can get up easily) they rest their paws flat on the ground.

In a more relaxed state (when feeding/holding their food with their forelegs, or just simply resting), they could also sit straight like humans; their bottoms lying flat on the ground with their back limbs stretched/relaxed forward. Panda bears and sloth bears use this sitting manner more often than the squat

---

Drawing Bears

position (since pandas usually hold a bamboo and have large round bottoms, making this position easier for them; and the sloth bears have relatively longer limbs).

Sloth Bear

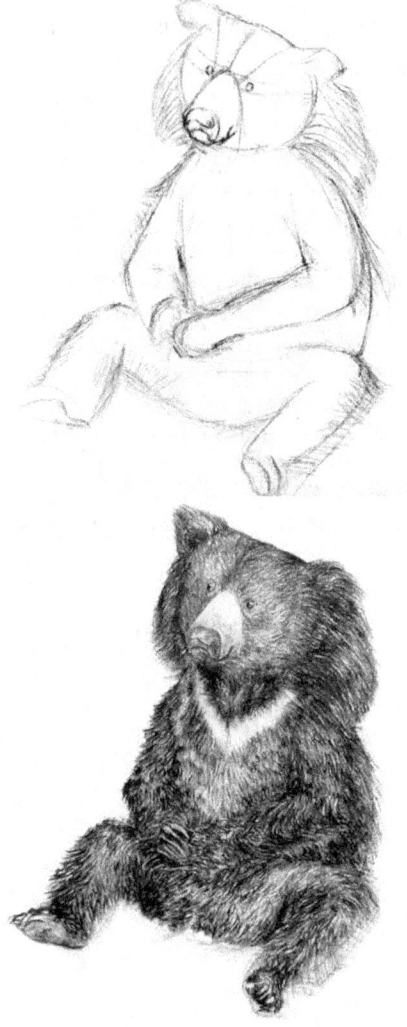

The individuals who first saw this bear taught of it as a bear-like sloth due to its physical features that highly resemble a sloth's, until it was recognized by experts as a subfamily of ancestral brown bears that made a convergent evolution. The sloth bear, also referred to as labiated bear/lip bear (to acknowledge its relatively long and flexible lower lip) or the Stickney bear is a little smaller compared to Asian black bears. Adults can grow from four to six feet; females are relatively smaller compared to males. Another reason for its mistaken identity at early times is due its usual diet. Sloth bears most often eat bugs and it is rare to see one hunting for other (smaller) mammals (if ever it sloth bear preyed on another mammal, it was probably provoked or in dire hunger).

The fur color of a sloth bear is often black (it is quite rare to see one with a reddish-brown/rusty color). It can be easily distinguished by its thick and long tousled fur with a mane around its nape and to its shoulders. Its ears are also covered with long fur (it's the only bear who has this characteristic) like an extension to its mane. The chest has a 'V' or 'Y' marking of white or pale-cream (which is also seen on sun bears and few Asian black bears). Sloth bears have lankier physique compared to those who are close to their size (Asian black bears). They have a relatively thicker muzzle and wider snout. Another easily distinguishable feature of this bear is its big paws with extensively long sickle-point nails.

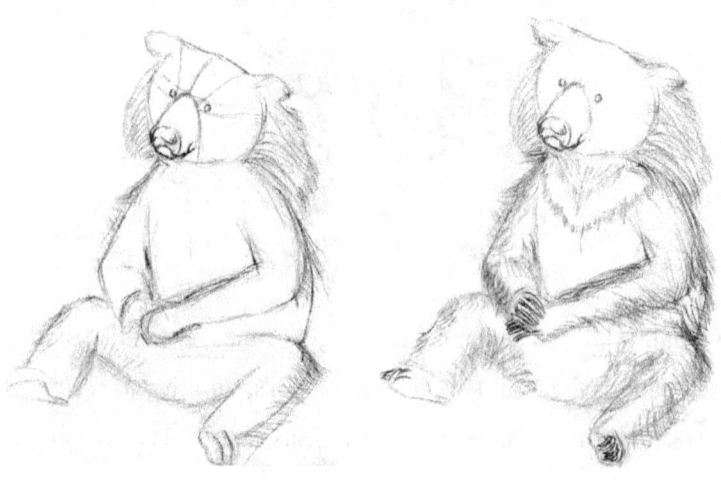

- Establish the size and position of the body.

Sketch the position of the bear. The extremities of the sloth bear are relatively long compared to the other bears. Use an oval to establish the size of its head (the head of a sloth bear is a little wide).

- Draw the Facial features.

Use reference lines to properly position the features. Make a cross reference mark to locate the center of the oval (according to the angle of the bear), and from that reference line, make another reference line in an upside-down 'Y' to establish the position of the muzzle. Find the center of the cylindrical shaped muzzle to locate the position of the nose.

- Establish the secondary details.

Draw the long claws of the sloth bear's paws. Establish the length of the mane's fur and the 'V' crest on the chest.

- Make a loose sketch of the fur.

Simply draw some lines to establish the directions of the hatches that will fill up the entire body of the bear, you will use this as a guide while you are applying several layers of thin hatches.

- Thicken the fur by following its line directions.

You are going to need thin short and fairly long hatches to establish the furry texture of the bear/subject. The layers of the hatches will be defined with different line darkness and lightness.

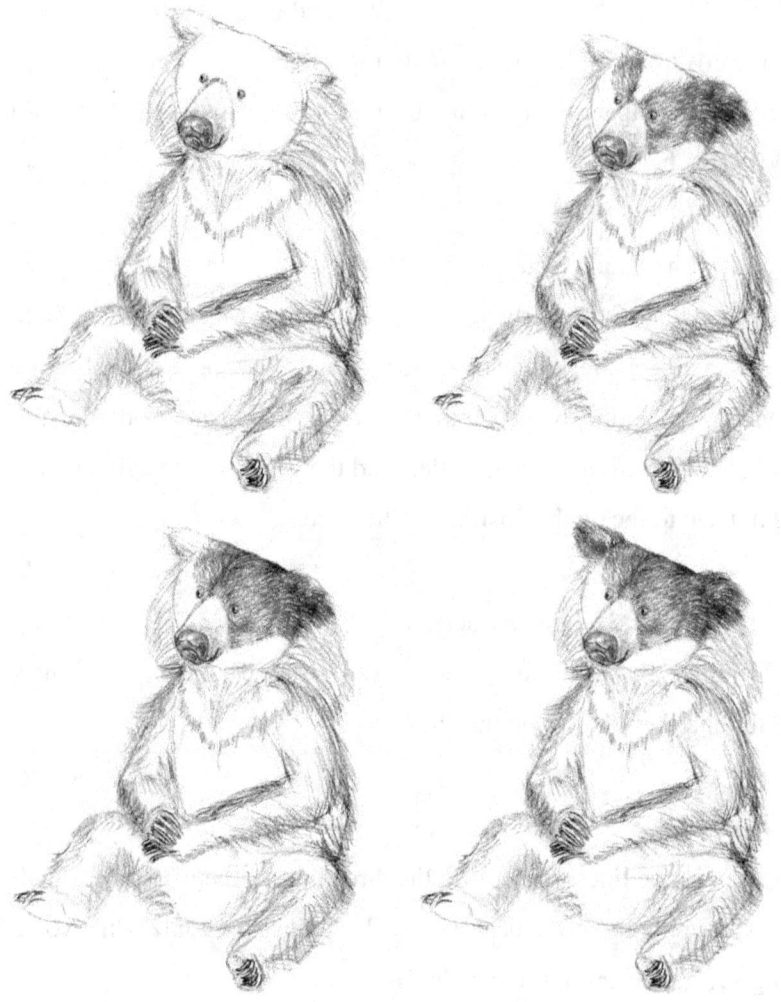

- Make the hatches flow with the head's dimensions.

Make a row of hatches in a 'V' shape coming from the eyes and to the ears. And then fill the entire space of the head by spreading the tight hatches to the top center of the head; and make another set of hatches across the cheeks to the mane.

- Fill the neck area and down to the upper side of the chest's white crest with curving lines spiking upwards and diagonally.

- Make several rows of hatches to fill the area of the body. From the lower side of the chest's crest, make rows of fur spiking diagonally, and as the row of line furs fill up the lower area, the hatches/lines should spike further downwards until the hatches are positioned vertically.

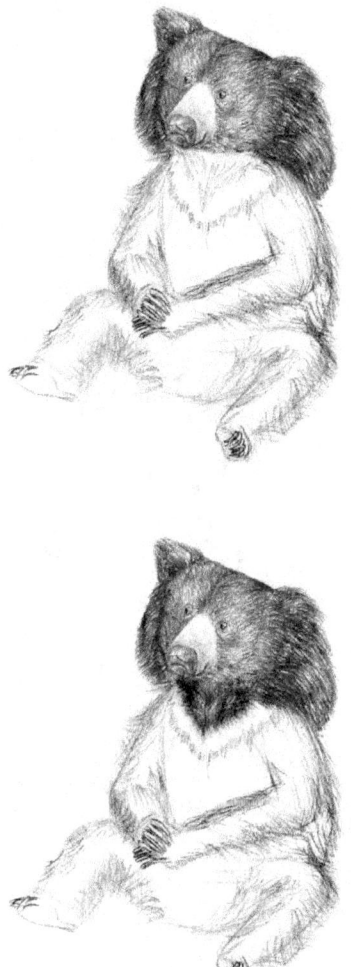

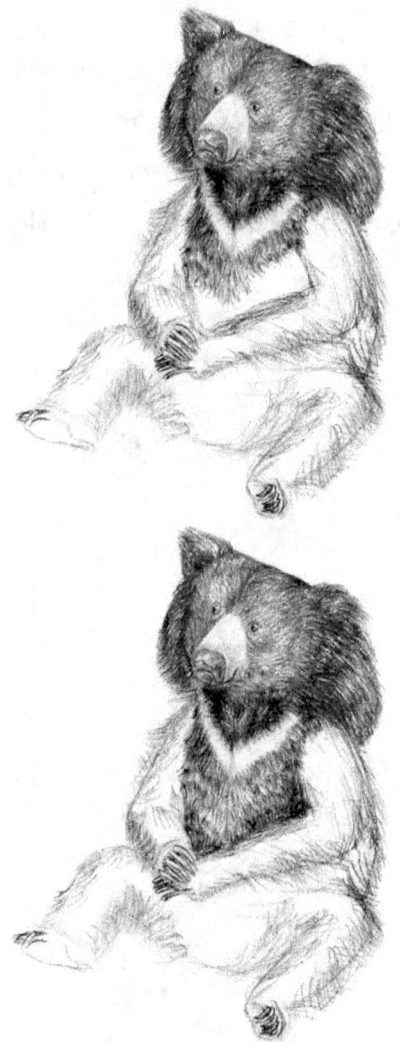

- Fill the back area and the arms of the bear.

Fill up the back area with curving fur lines that goes with its sloping plane.

The fur of the subject's arm are quite unruly; to portray this, apply several hatches that spike out from the base (extending outwards the arms' outline).

Make several rows of tight hatches with relatively different lengths that flow with the contour shape of the arm, most of the hatches should point downwards (if the base is positioned vertically). As the hatches reach the edge of the base, spike the lines further sideway (making/curving the vertical hatches diagonally from the base).

Do the same process to the legs. As the hatches reach the crotch, the diagonal lines should gradually flip further (making the diagonal hatches turn horizontally).

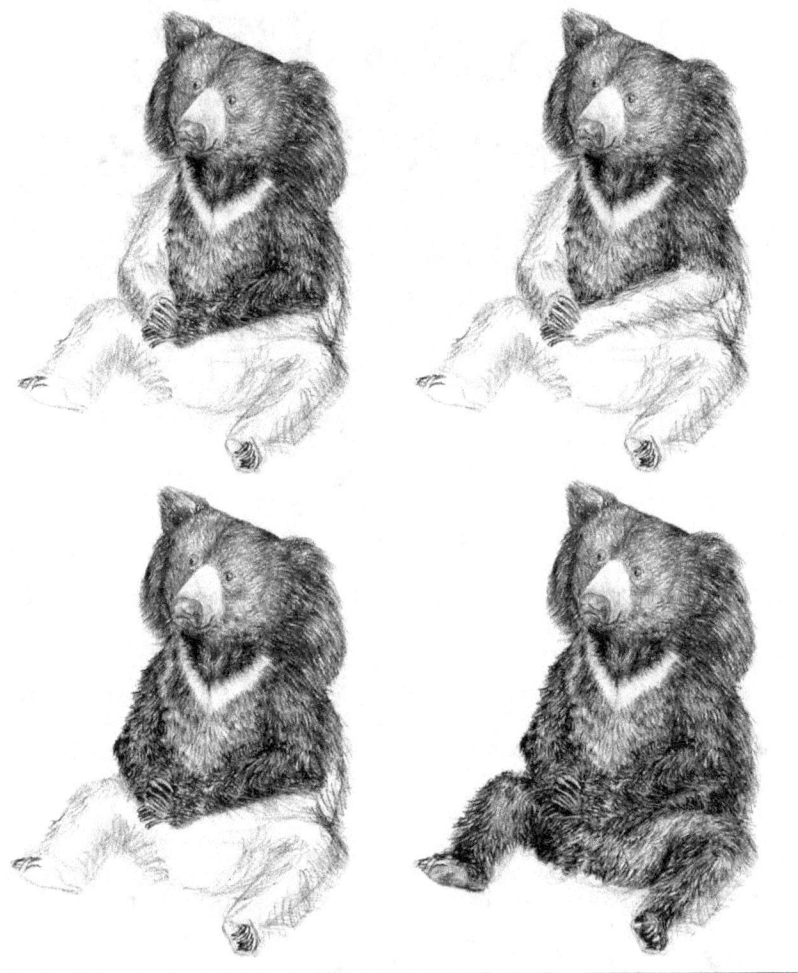

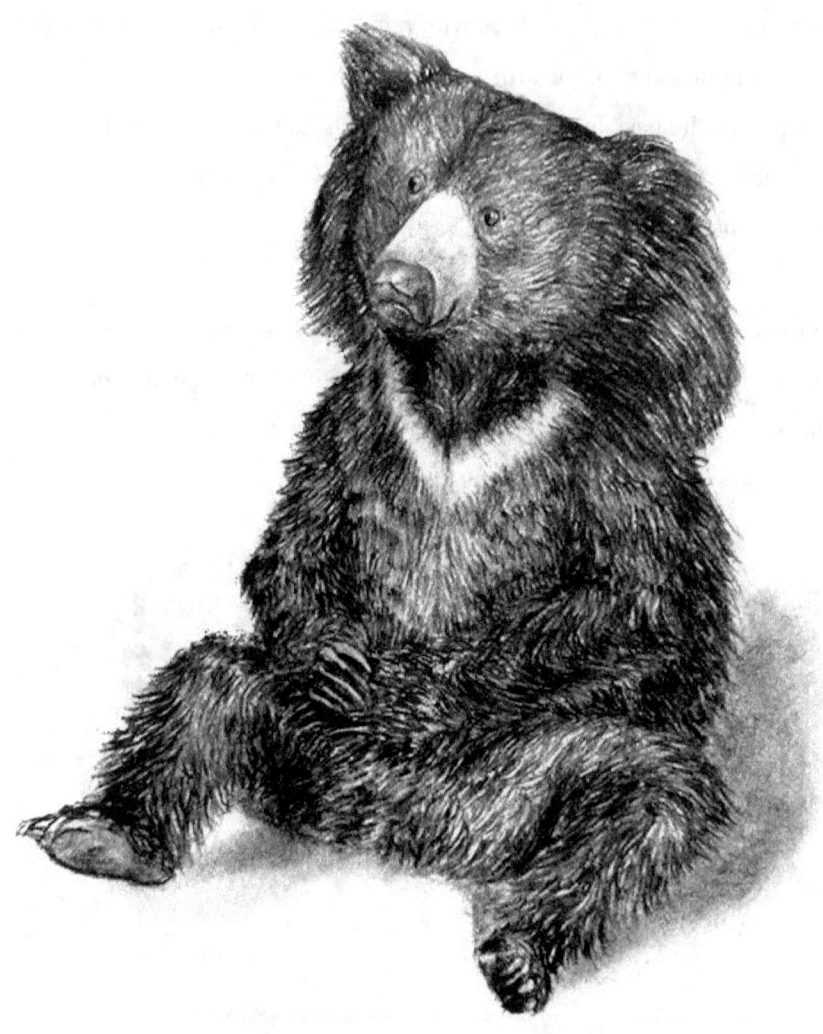

This bear sniffs his way on the forest ground to locate bugs' nests. And like a sloth, it uses its long thick nails to dig out the bugs from their mounds and suck them out. It can climb the trees to fetch some fruits, and find its favorite snack which is honeycomb (thus, the name honey bear). Sloth bears are quite noisy creatures, they make different kinds of noises when they eat, call for a mate and at the time of mating, when frightened or defending its spot. And it is said that there are times when they would make noises for no apparent reason (it's probably the reason why locals also call them the jungle jokers).

Giant Panda

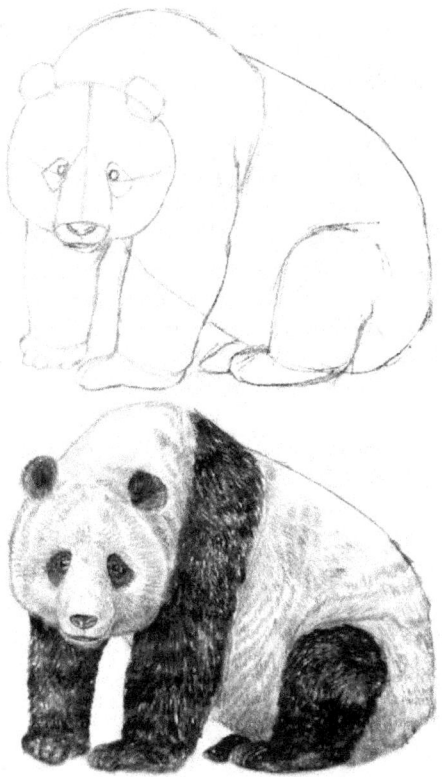

The giant panda is probably the most widely desired kind of bear among any others. It black and white coat and round head make it look simply adorable, as if it's just a big cuddly stuffed toy. Giant pandas, like its far relative (red/lesser panda), were also mistaken for something else.

Like the red panda, there were arguments if whether it should be classified to the family of raccoons or bear, until they discovered that it is a descendant of the spectacled bear genus.

A panda bear is coated with fairly short fur of black and white (although there are kinds/subspecies that have brown hues). The abdomen and most of its head is white (with black-furred ears, and black spots on both eyes). The black portions on its body are the limbs. With the black coat on its forelimbs/arms extending around the chest and on its back.

It is common for panda bears to have a fairly huge physique because they eat a huge amount of bamboos regularly (resulting to approximately forty defecations each day). The shape of the head is round because of the thick muscular jaw. The muzzle is fairly thick, with black oval snout and black lips.

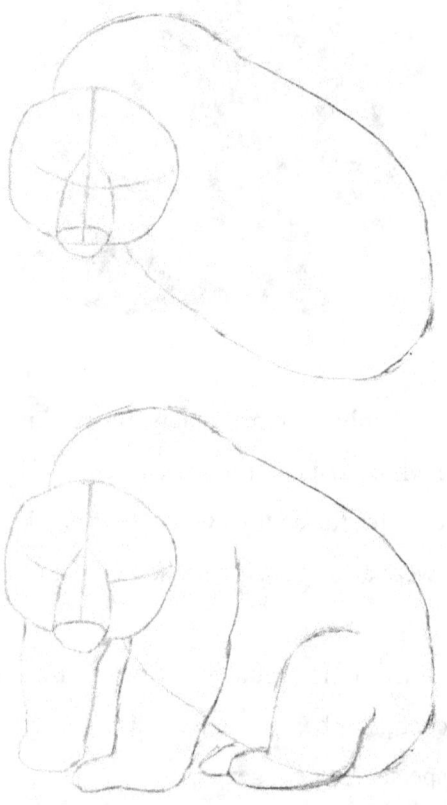

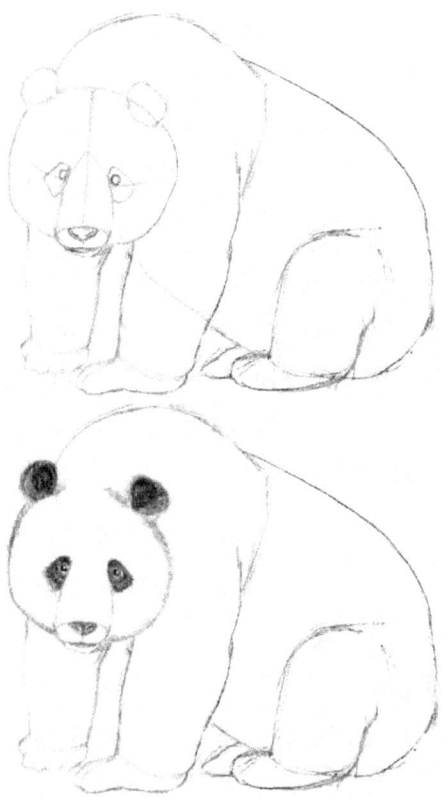

- Establish the basic figure of the giant panda.

Convey the figure of the bear with basic shapes. The thick body of a giant panda can be easily established with an irregularly shaped oval; the area right above the forelegs should be more prominent (to convey the shoulders) compared to the outline of the rest (belly, back and bottom). The head of the giant panda is basically round. In this kind of sitting position, the level of the head should be lowered down.

On a sitting gesture, the hind limbs are folded, so the length should be shorter than the fore limbs (with an outline like an upside-down 'L' or 'J'). Establish the division of the white areas from the black (of the body), the limbs are usually black/dark-furred, the area of the chest and around the back (right about the level of the nape). The paws of a giant panda are big, matching its thick arms and body.

- Define the facial features.

Use reference lines to easily place the facial features. Place the cross reference mark to locate the sphere front center of the sphere/head and establish the position of the head. Make a semi-cylindrical shape for the muzzle. In this angle, the outline of the muzzle should begin right above the horizontal reference line. Use the vertical line to find the center of the muzzle and properly place the triangular nose and the exposed outline of the lower lip.

- Start conveying the fur of the head.

Follow the contour figure of the round head; from the center, start with fairly short hatches with each rows arching along with the spherical dimensions of the plane, as the row of hatch lines get nearer to the edges, gradually lengthen the hatches. Leave a gap between each curved rows. The surface of the head can be filled with more or less three to four rows of hatch lines.

- Darken the black areas/spots of the head.

Places some hatches right above the level of the muzzle (the gap between the eyes). These hatches should also be arced like the others. Place some vertical hatches on the muzzle to describe its slightly foreshortened form/perspective. You should only place the hatches bon the lower/nearer portion of the muzzle and the areas near the edges.

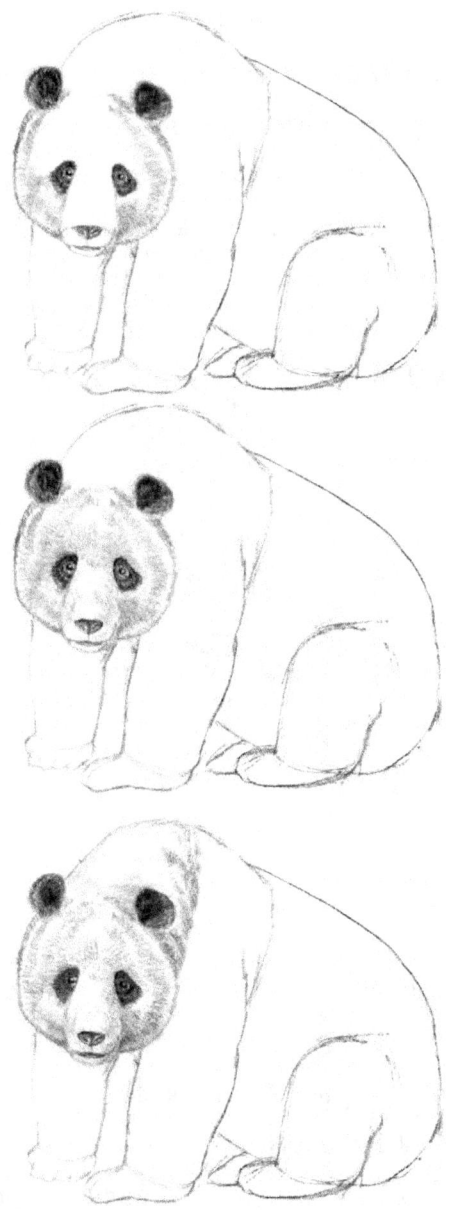

- Use a fairly light and thin lines with different lengths to effectively portray a bright/white fur.

In this case, you have to portray the white fur with a pencil; basically, you are going to depict the shades created by the fur, so the grey tone has to be light and properly rowed across the contour figure of the subject.

As you get to a brighter area, gradually loosen the gaps between each hatches and lighten the line strokes. The brightest points/portions should be the back/upper portion of the body, the shoulder, and the small area on top of the muzzle. Thus, the hatches should gradually be closer and darker as it gets to the lower area (since the planes are curved, it should appear darker).

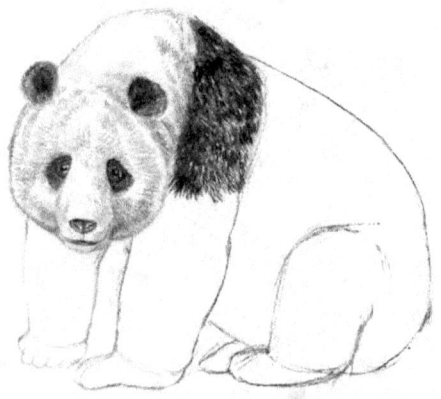

- Define the dark fur.

For the area with black fur coating, the short lines should be thick and heavy. Fill the areas with tightly close rows of hatch lines nearly overlapping the ends of each line strokes. Use heavy and short hand strokes and don't leave any gap in between the rows of the line marks. This would create a thick layer of dark short hatches with few subtle highlights. Gradually slant the short lines as you get nearer to the edges of the base.

Just like with the lighter and thinner hatches, the black short hatches should also depict the contour dimensions of the plane.

- Establish the light fur lines from the belly and up to the back. Make several rows of short light hatch lines bending along with the round dimensions from the belly and up to the back of the bear.

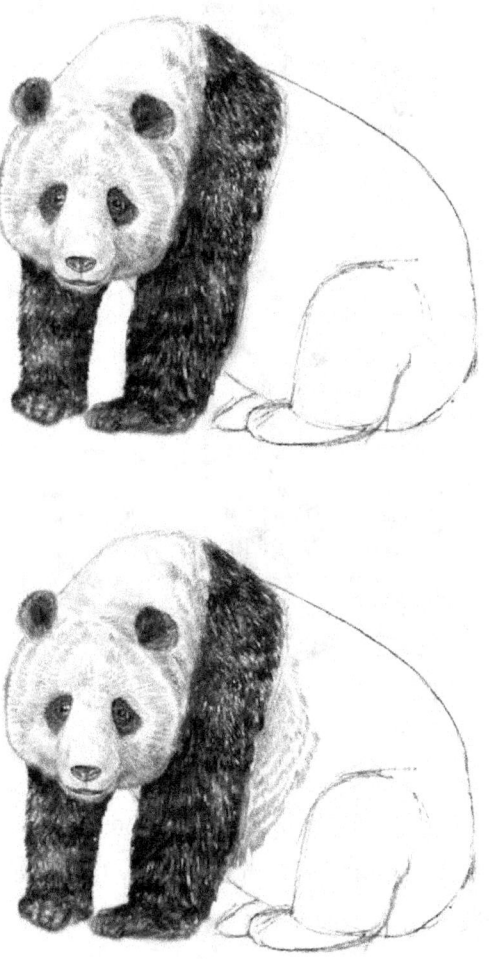

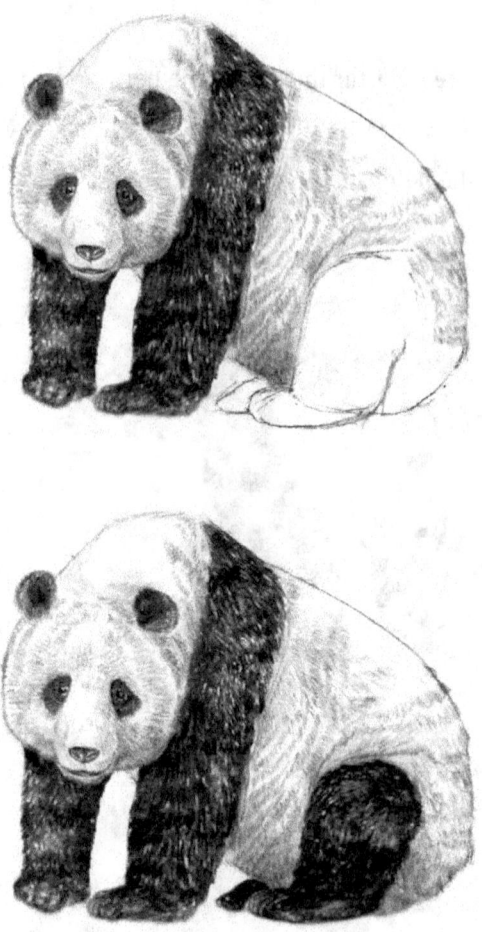

To depict a subtle fold on the surface, change the position of the curves row of hatches. Some rows should come horizontally from the outline of the outline/beneath the forelimbs, these rows of short lines should join or flow with the other rows of coming vertically from the area of the belly.

Apply some row of hatches following the line rows of the head's outline, take note that the area is bright and less curvy compared to the dimensions of the belly.

- Establish the fur on the bottom area of the bear.

The row of hatches coming underneath the bottom of the bear should be relatively closer to each other. The hatches at the bottom are slightly darker. Create some darker lines strokes especially on the area at the bottom. And just like the other row of hatches, these rows should also arc with the dimensions of plane.

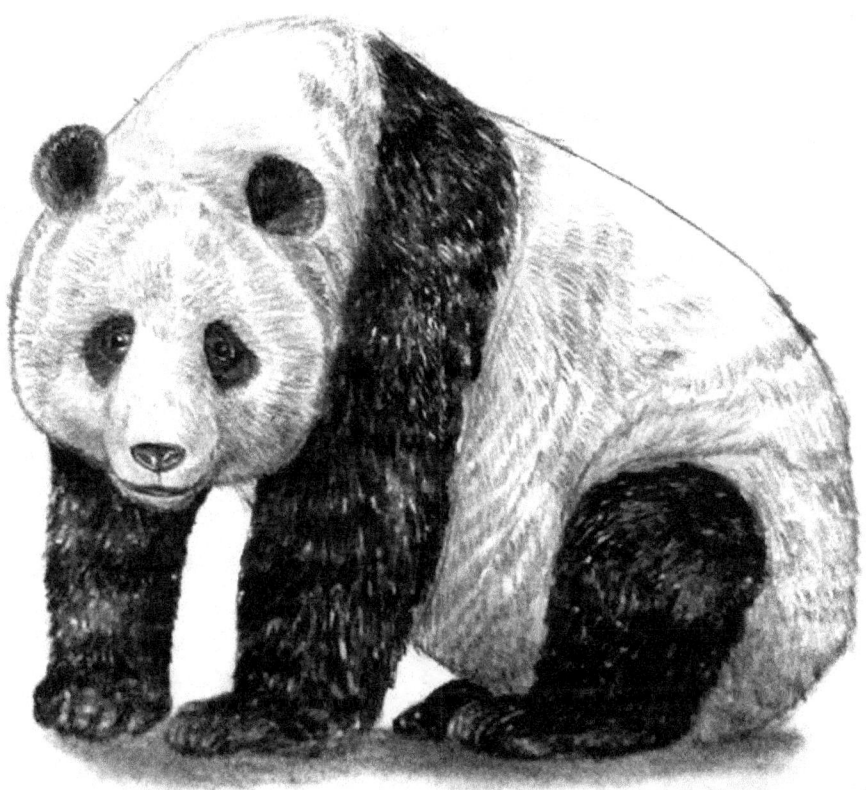

The giant panda was called the 'bear cat" due to its vertical iris that resembles a cat's. In fact, a lot of names were given to this bear that incorporates it to felines. In old Chinese literature works, it was referred to as 'Mo' which means 'white leopard', and 'Zouyo' that was described as an herbivorous white tiger having black spotting. Even its traditional/old local name 'Dàxióngmāo' means big bearcat. It was also called the mottled bear or particolored bear, spotted bear and bamboo bear. Giant pandas are considered as an endangered species due to (as expected) illegal hunting and habitat loss because of inevitable modernization, and their poor reproduction habit. Pandas would only mate once a year, and the female could only produce two cubs. Only one of the two newborns often survives. Thankfully, this bear species is highly valued and a lot of efforts are being given for its conservation.

Black Bear

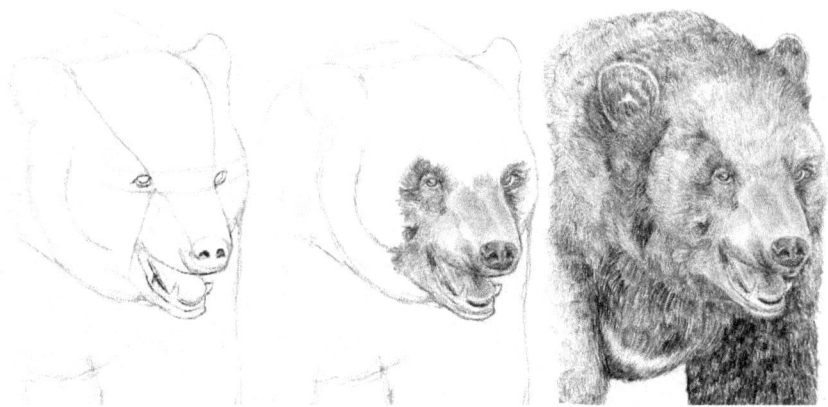

The American black bear or the Ursus Americanus inhabits the forest grounds and Woodland terrains of North America. It is typically a medium-sized type of bear. In North America, it is known to be the smallest bear species, but the largest of its kind can be compared to a grizzly bear. The growth in height and mass of the black bears depends on the climate and amount of food available at the area it lives on. Its average body height ranges from forty-seven to eighty inches. Females are relatively larger compared to males.

Although this bear species is referred to as black bear, it does not mean that all of them are black. There are others with fur colors ranging from different values of brown and white. The cinnamon black bear (as the name suggests) has a reddish brown coat, while the Kermode or locally known as the spirit bear is a greyish white furred black bear (sometimes creamish-brown).

Most of the other black bears (as the name says) are black or black with few taints of dark brown, some of them have white markings on their chest (like its relative, the Asian black bear or Sun bears). Their thick muzzles are dark-brown to cream in color. The muzzles of females are relatively narrower compared to the males'. The head profile of a black bear is less curvy compared to a brown bear's. It has less-prominent shoulders than the other types of bears it can be compared with (perhaps by size), and it has relatively longer ears that is more oval-shaped than round.

It is much easier to construct the details if you understand how the planes build up the figure when drawing a head of a bear.

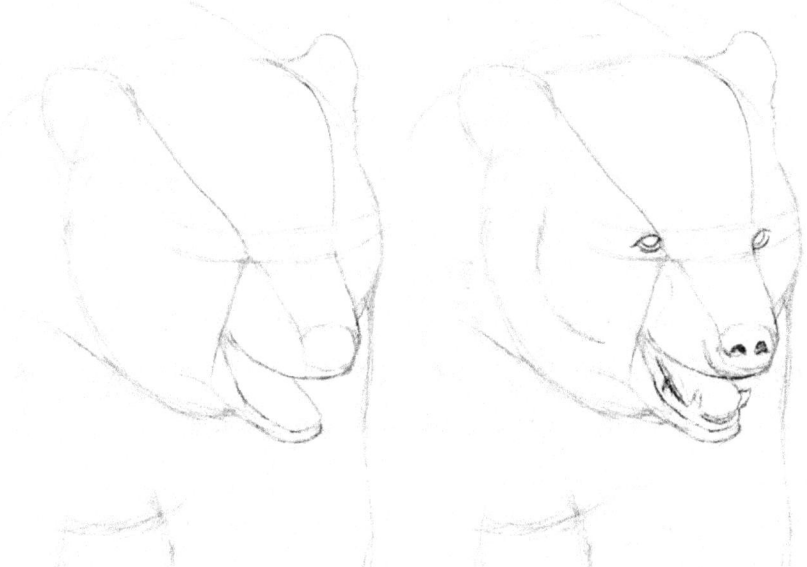

- Combined with some reference lines and establishment of each planes, build the basic figure of the bear's head.

The triangular pen can be used to establish the form of the head from the crown/top of the head, and down to the upper area of the muzzle. Using this plane, establish the side of the muzzle. And base on the plane for the side of the muzzle, place horizontal lines to establish the alignment and placing of the eyes. Make a reference line for the opening of the mouth.

- Using the reference lines, establish the facial features of the bear. Draw the eyes, ears and nose of the bear. And then draw the teeth and the tongue for the opened mouth.

- Clean up the drawing by erasing the reference lines and outlines of the planes.

- Shade the muzzle.

Apply some fairly thin layer of gray tone to the muzzle. Blend/smear the shades to loosen any recognizable line marks. Leave a faint highlight at the center of the muzzle's top plane, and brighter (lesser shade) portions at the nearest sides.

- Establish the fur with fairly short hatches.

You have to be patient to be able to portray the fur coating of the bear effectively, there is no shortcut for this step, it is made this way so you can properly adjust and arrange each line that portrays each fur.

Convey the fur of the bear's head by applying several layers of hatches. The direction of the hatches should flow with the contour dimensions of the head.

Few hatches should spike out of the row it follows (ends of the hatches slightly curving or slanting), this will portray the furry texture effectively.

The portion of the eyes are slightly sloped inwards, so you have to establish this change in plane with the direction of the hatches surrounding it. Apply some fairly dark and short hatches around both eyes.

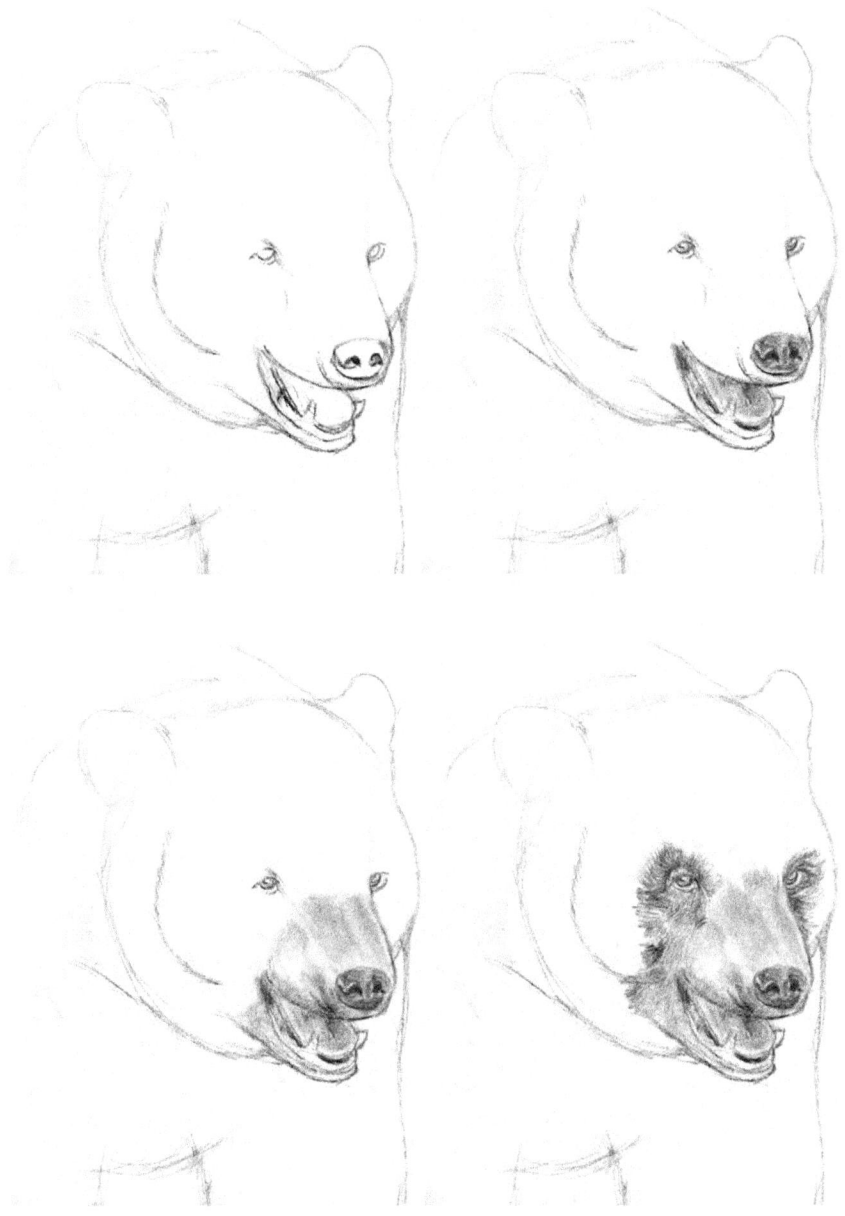

- The direction of the rowed hatches should change according to the planes of the head.

Take note of the head's angle. Basically, most of the hatch lines should point backwards from the muzzle. The side of the muzzle contains subtle change in planes, establish this with at least 2 to 3 rows of curving hatches spiking off the direction of the rows of lines.

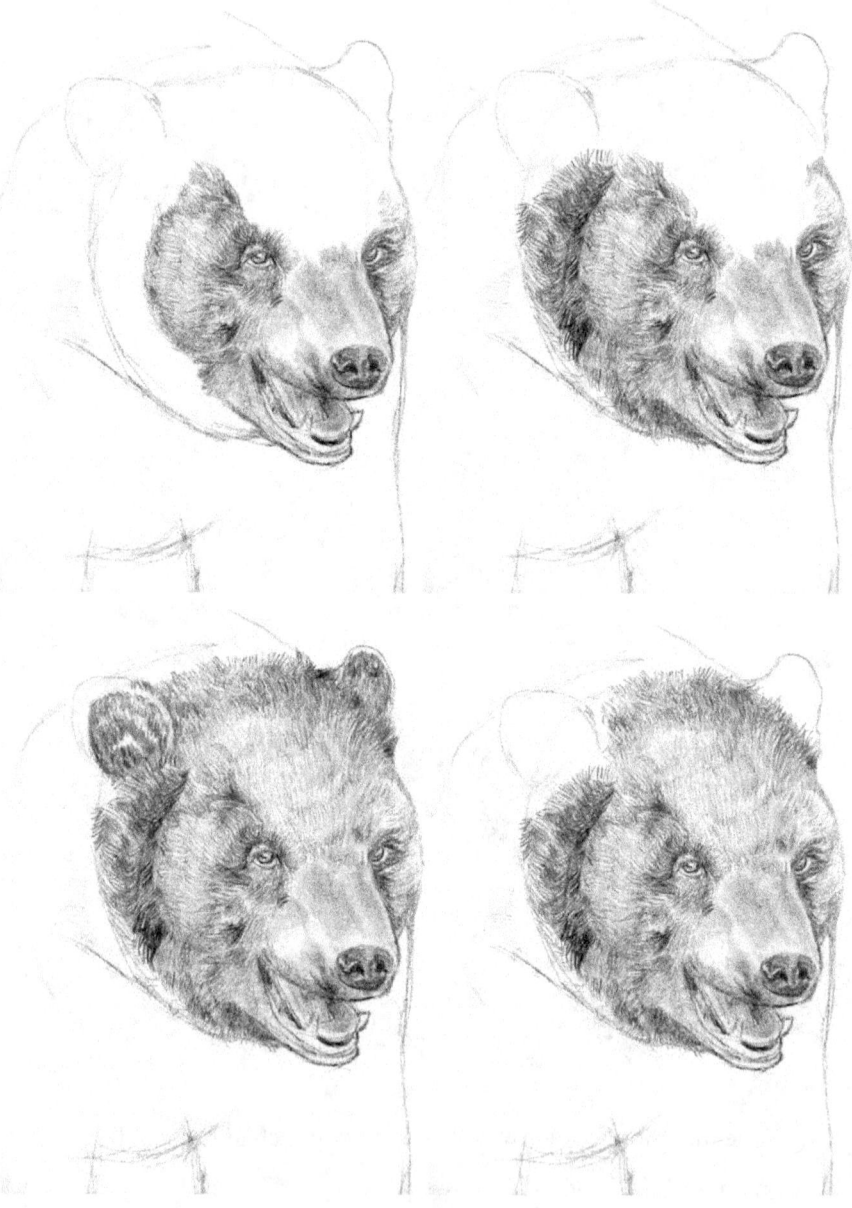

- Initiate the same method for applying the fur of the body.

Curve the rows of hatches with the cylindrical shape of the legs. The slope of the body (down to the crest and further) should point towards the farther side of the body.

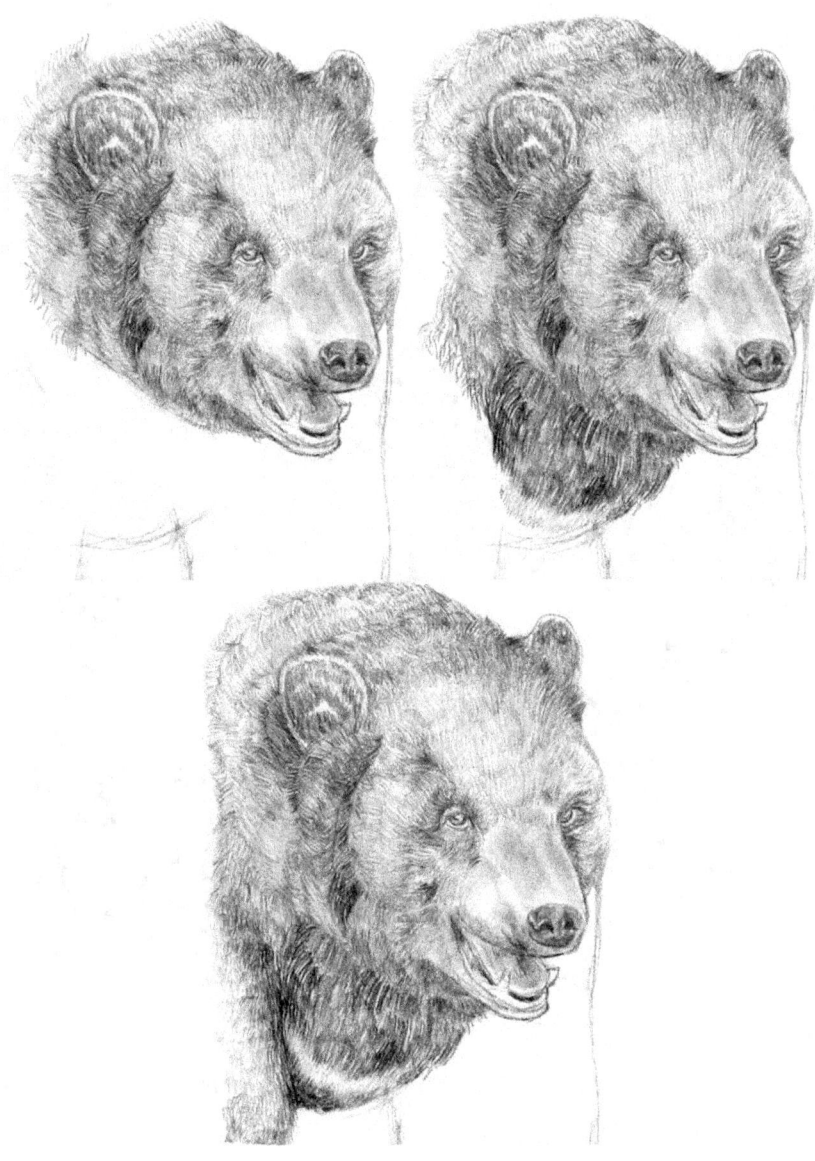

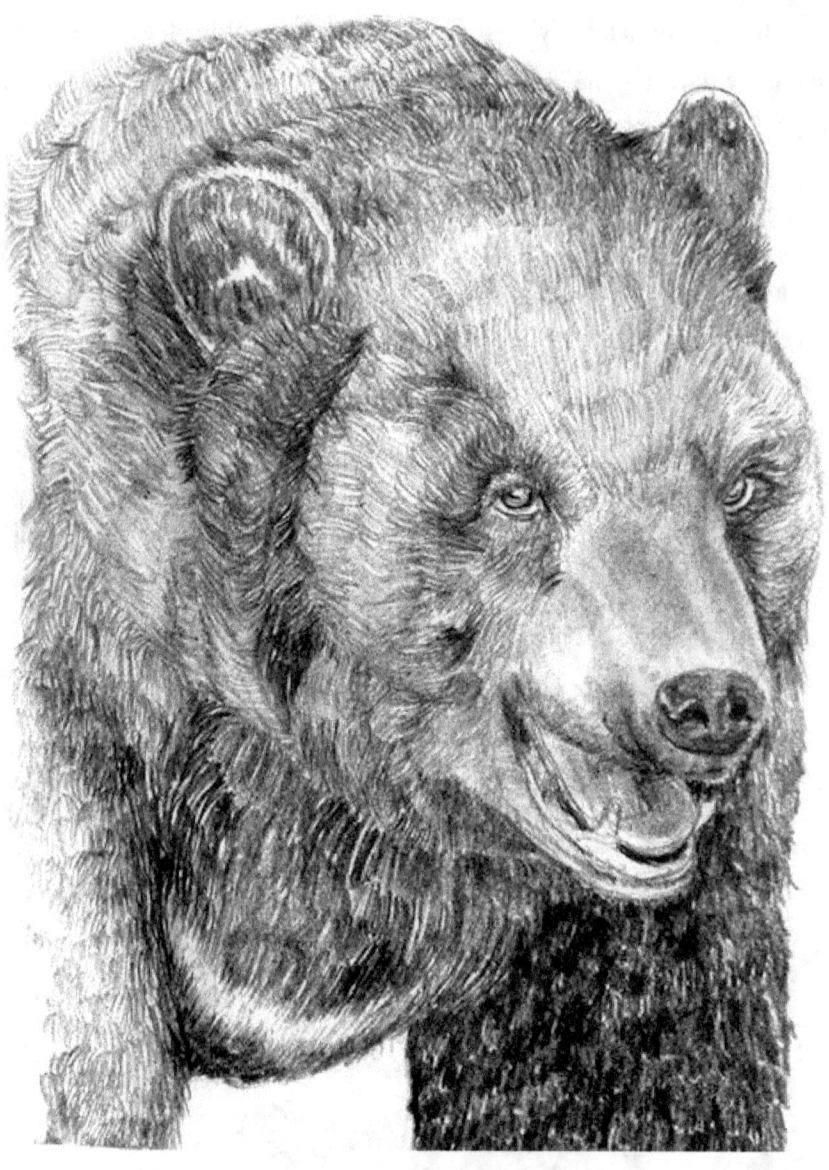

Black bears are commonly seen on thick and undisturbed forests, but they also migrate to other areas to avoid being preyed upon by larger mammals (due to its size, the cubs are often hunted by wolves and other bears) and to find food. The population of this bear species is quite big and it is far from being extinct.

Growling Bear

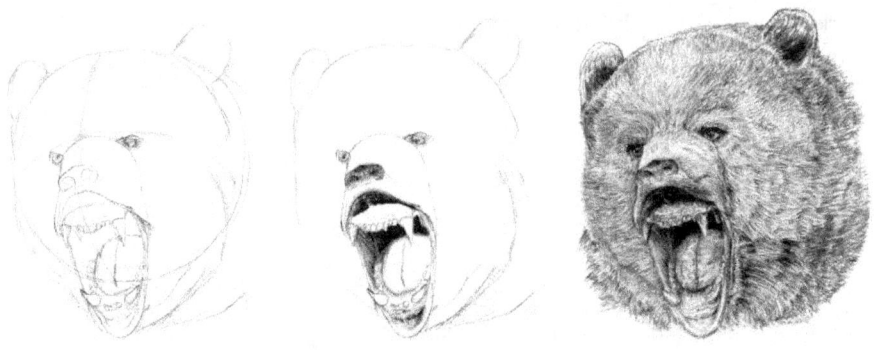

The only difficulty when drawing a growling bear is expressing the perspective/angle of its head and features properly. Open the mouth of the bear widely so the bear can show its powerful fangs; show the gum and the thick tongue. It is much easier if you are going to base on an image so you can easily observe if there is something missing in your drawing.

- Start with a sphere/circle, and then establish the angle of the head by identifying the center with a cross reference mark.

Use the circle to easily establish the shape of the head. Use the reference mark to properly establish the position of the eyes, nose and the upper lip. Use the upper lip to properly establish the outline of the lower lip.

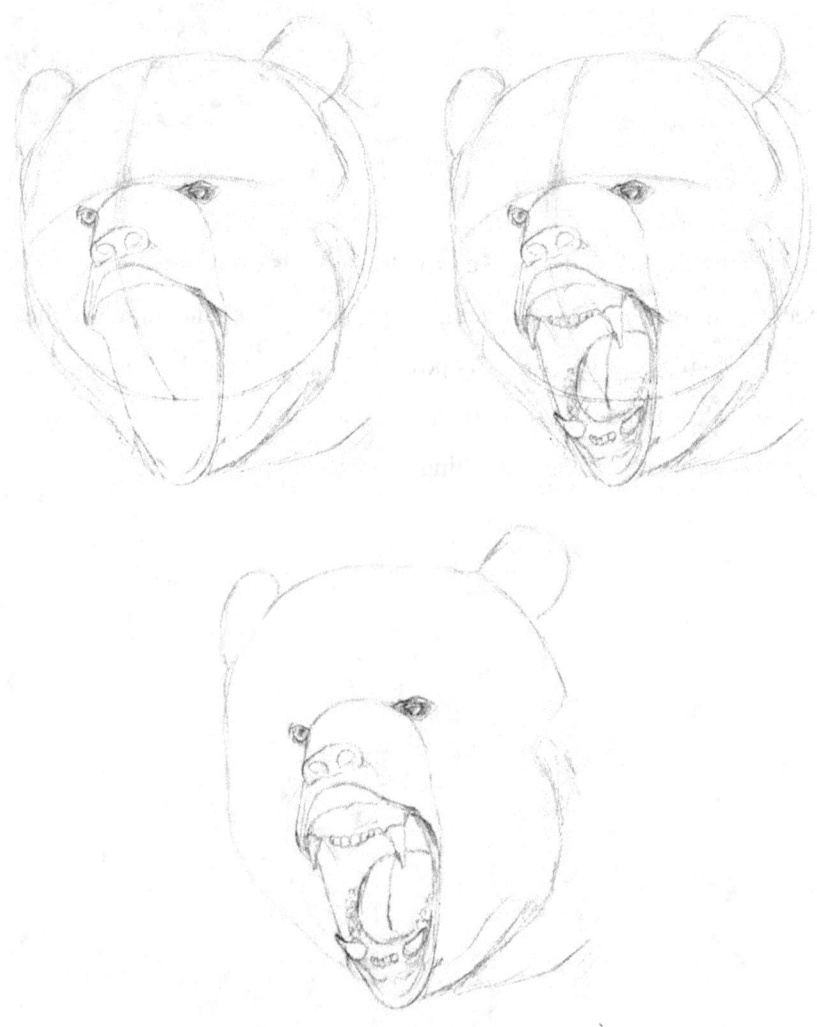

- Draw the details of the mouth.

Start with the details of the upper portion; the underside of the upper lip is partially exposed. The gum and the teeth are of the upper area are basically arced. Needless to say, the lower teeth should be in a 'U' shape formation. Find the center of the upper set of teeth and the middle lining of the tongue using the vertical reference mark you used to establish the center of the head.

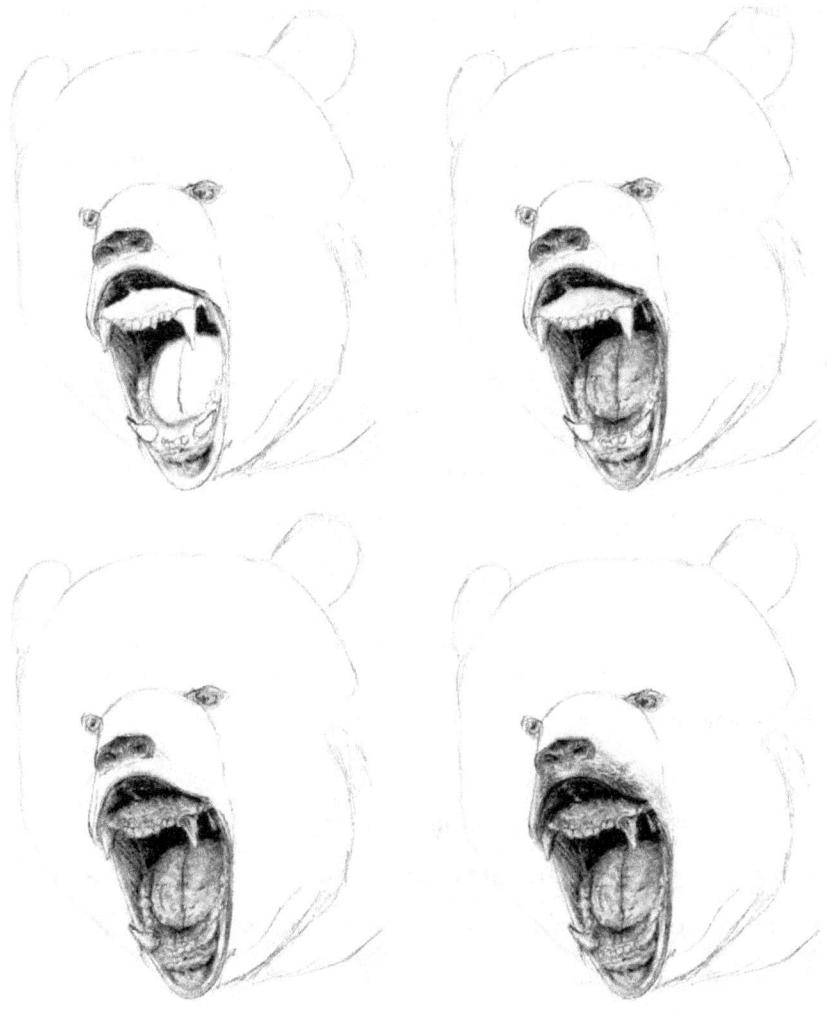

- Start applying the shades of the mouth.

Take note of the tone values (level of brightness and darkness) you apply to each sections. The underside of the upper lip should be second darkest value of the mouth gradation; it should not be as dark as the farther/inner areas of the mouth, but it should not be as light as the tone of the gums.

The subtle details on the gums can be conveyed with highlights, and the faint linings on the exposed inner side of the mouth can be established with subtle marks (for the slopes of the tongue) and the side of the mouth. Be careful when you apply the shading, use small scribbling strokes so you can easily control what portions should have a lighter tone to define the detailing, such as the stretch of the flesh and the linings of the gums. Use light hand strokes to shade the small areas with darker tones; right under the upper lip and underneath the lower gum and the tongue.

- Define the shades of the eyes and the nose.

Think of (like three rings) overlaid circles with different shade values when shading the eyes, whit the center of the iris having the darkest value. Take note of the highlight (for the gloss) when darkening the eyes.

The top area of the nose should have the darkest value for this part. The shades should be coming from the sides. Apply a few stippling to define the texture of the nose.

- Portray the small amount of fur on the muzzle.

The muzzle does not have long strands of fur aside from the few whiskers which are barely observable. This can be easily done with hatches of different weight and length.

For the direction of each hatch lines, remember that each should point backwards from the nearer side it occupies.

As the faint hatches go around the curve of the muzzle, it should gradually point downwards (like a vertical hatch gradually sliding diagonally). The fur covering nearest portion/curve of the muzzle where the whiskers reside are faintly darker, but the fur lines barely strike outwards from the base/surface. To convey the surface of this area, we are going to use faint line marks, shades and highlights to establish the fur lines; use a combination of light smearing shade and a combination of small scribbling shades.

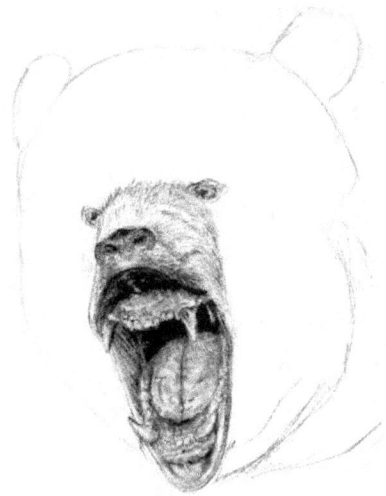

- Use some slightly curved hatches to establish the fur on the face. The fur of a bear fluffs when they are growling, technically the hatches that establishes each fur lines are curved outwards.

Aside from the slopes and sudden changes in plane on the structure of the face, the hatch lines have a pattern that you could follow to properly portray the fur coat.

- The 'V' pattern of the fur from the area of the eyebrows and up across the ears, following the curved hatches establishing the slope of the eyehole.
- The hatches flowing and pointing backwards to cover the forehead and the top of the head.
- The hatches coming from at the sides of the muzzle, positioned downwards and slightly curving its lower end sideward, as the lines reach the lower area of the face, the vertical lines would slant and turn diagonally (following the flow of the arcing hatches).
- The hatches at the near edge of the face are pointing outwards, thus, most of them are position horizontally.
- All of the remaining fur lines on other sections left simply bends with and flow with the direction of the other fur lines they are joined with.
- Darken the other rows of hatches to establish its layered form. And darken the other areas that should appear darker, such as the side of the head with the longest fur lines, the inner areas of the ear, and the bordering outline of the head from the neck.

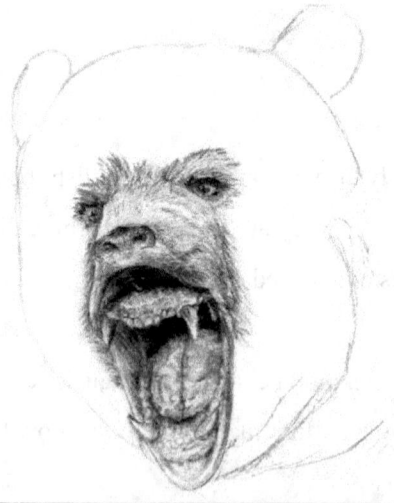

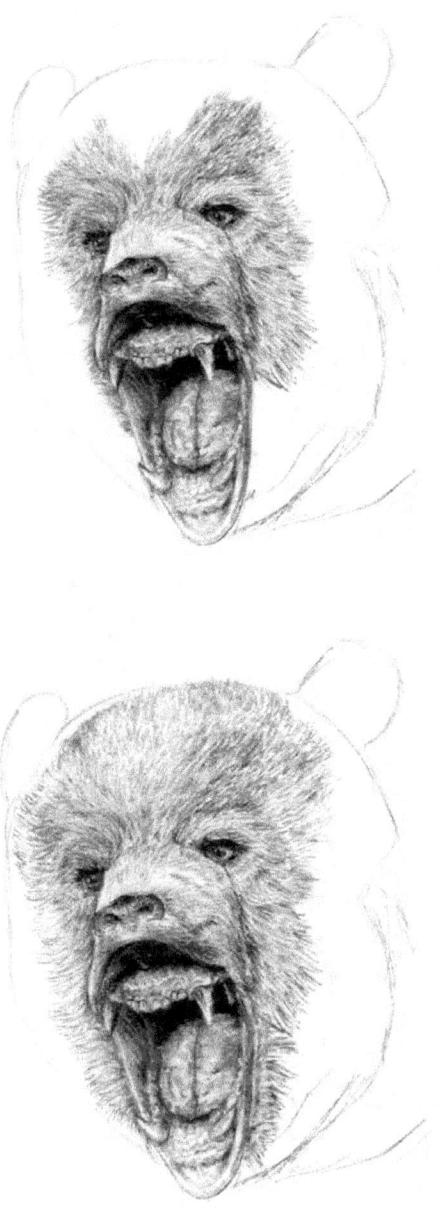

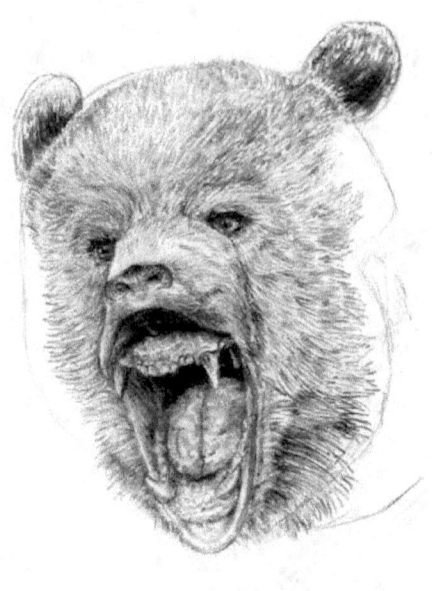

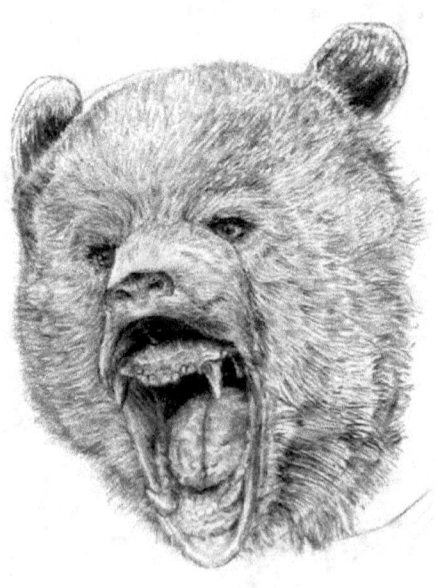

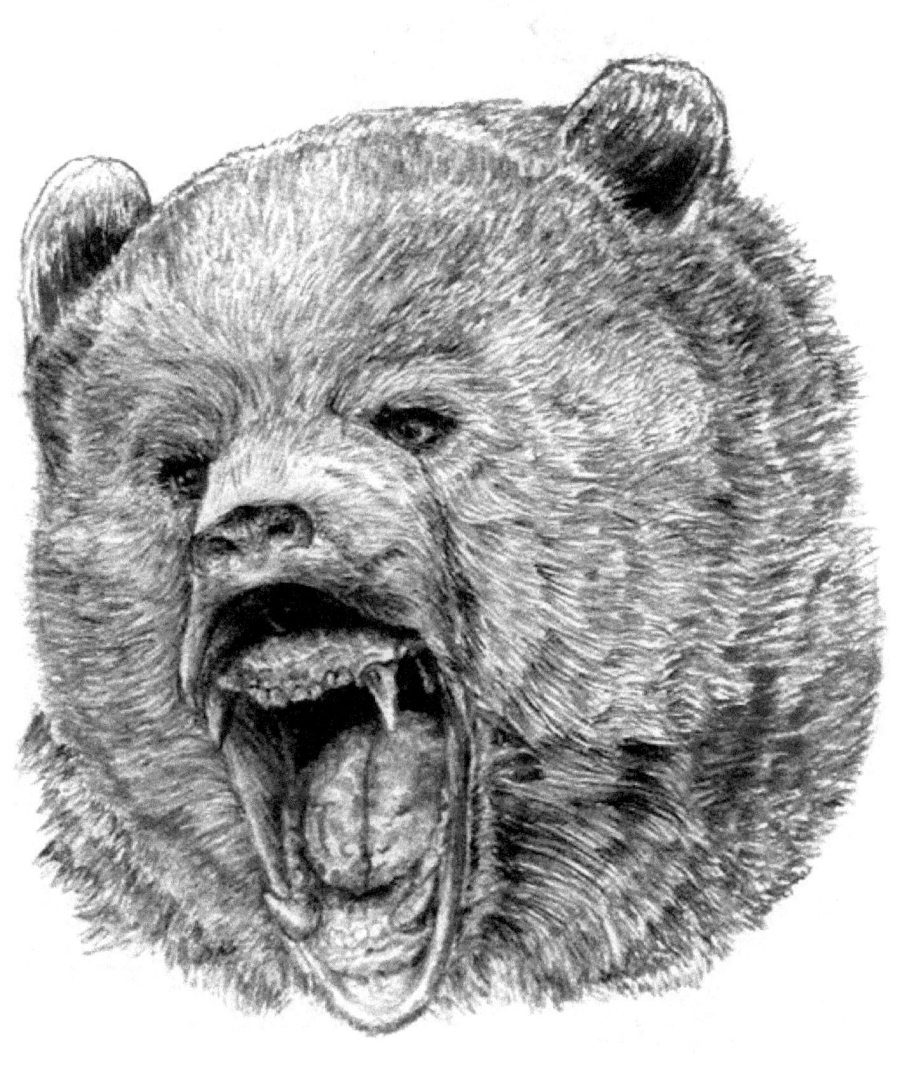

Thank you for reading.

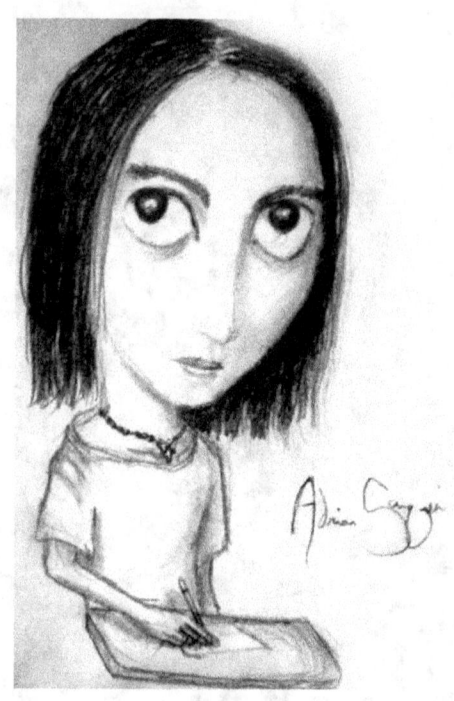

Author Bio

Adrian Sanqui

Check out some of my other books:

Manual Drawing for the Absolute Beginner

Learn to Draw People

Learn to Draw Cartoons

Learn to Draw Super Heroes

Learn to Draw Faces and Portraits

Learn to Draw Caricatures

Learn to Draw Animals in Pencil

How to Draw Lizards

Drawing Cartoon Animals for the Beginner

Drawing Insects for Beginners

Drawing Birds for Beginners

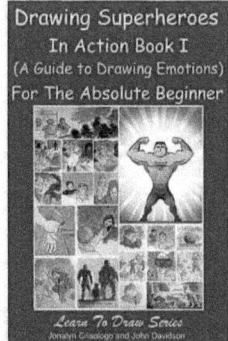

Drawing Superheroes In Action Book I (A Guide to Drawing Emotions) For The Absolute Beginner — Learn To Draw Series — Jonalyn Crisologo and John Davidson

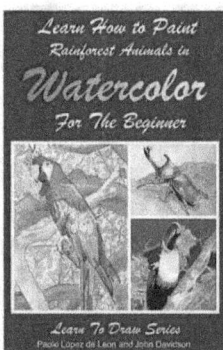

Learn How to Paint Rainforest Animals in Watercolor For The Beginner — Learn To Draw Series — Paolo Lopez de Leon and John Davidson

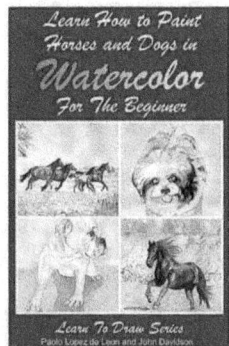

Learn How to Paint Horses and Dogs in Watercolor For The Beginner — Learn To Draw Series — Paolo Lopez de Leon and John Davidson

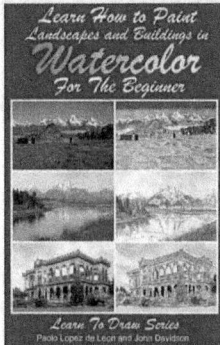

Learn How to Paint Landscapes and Buildings in Watercolor For The Beginner — Learn To Draw Series — Paolo Lopez de Leon and John Davidson

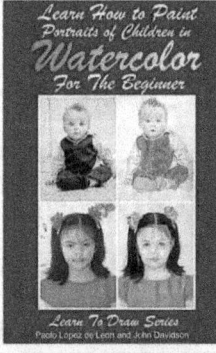

Learn How to Paint Portraits of Children in Watercolor For The Beginner — Learn To Draw Series — Paolo Lopez de Leon and John Davidson

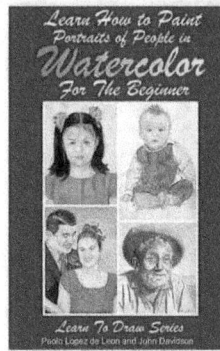

Learn How to Paint Portraits of People in Watercolor For The Beginner — Learn To Draw Series — Paolo Lopez de Leon and John Davidson

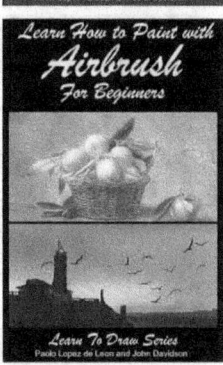

Learn How to Paint with Airbrush For Beginners — Learn To Draw Series — Paolo Lopez de Leon and John Davidson

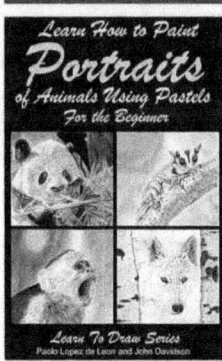

Learn How to Paint Portraits of Animals Using Pastels For the Beginner — Learn To Draw Series — Paolo Lopez de Leon and John Davidson

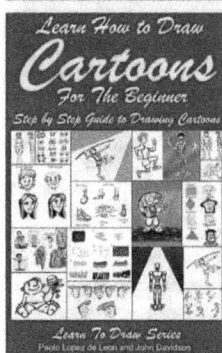

Learn How to Draw Cartoons For The Beginner Step by Step Guide to Drawing Cartoons — Learn To Draw Series — Paolo Lopez de Leon and John Davidson

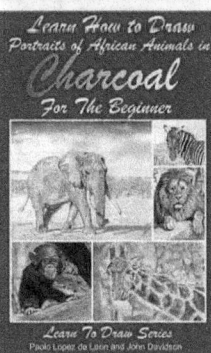

Learn How to Draw Portraits of African Animals in Charcoal For The Beginner — Learn To Draw Series — Paolo Lopez de Leon and John Davidson

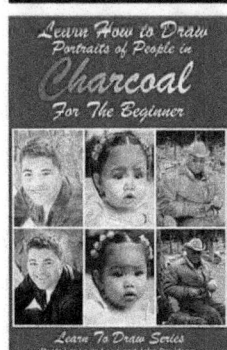

Learn How to Draw Portraits of People in Charcoal For The Beginner — Learn To Draw Series — Paolo Lopez de Leon and John Davidson

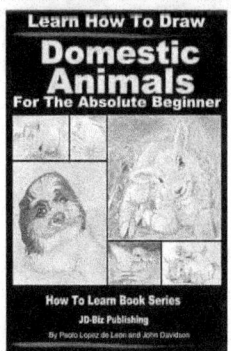

Learn How To Draw Domestic Animals For The Absolute Beginner — How To Learn Book Series — JD-Biz Publishing — By Paolo Lopez de Leon and John Davidson

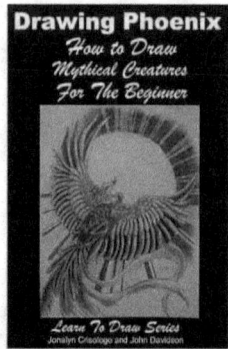

Drawing Phoenix
How to Draw
Mythical Creatures
For The Beginner

Learn To Draw Series
Jonalyn Crisologo and John Davidson

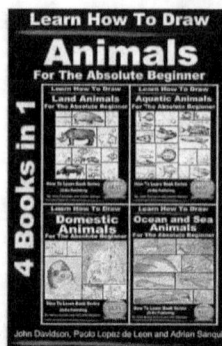

Learn How To Draw
Animals
For The Absolute Beginner
4 Books in 1

Learn How To Draw
Land Animals
For The Absolute Beginner

Learn How To Draw
Aquatic Animals
For The Absolute Beginner

Learn How To Draw
Domestic Animals
For The Absolute Beginner

Learn How To Draw
Ocean and Sea Animals
For The Absolute Beginner

John Davidson, Paolo Lopez de Leon and Adrian Sanqui

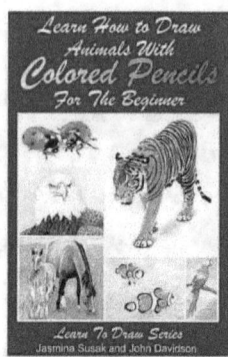

Learn How to Draw
Animals With
Colored Pencils
For The Beginner

Learn To Draw Series
Jasmina Susak and John Davidson

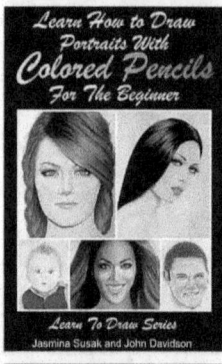

Learn How to Draw
Portraits With
Colored Pencils
For The Beginner

Learn To Draw Series
Jasmina Susak and John Davidson

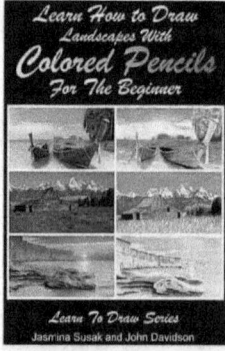

Learn How to Draw
Landscapes With
Colored Pencils
For The Beginner

Learn To Draw Series
Jasmina Susak and John Davidson

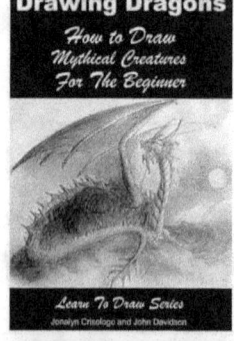

Drawing Dragons
How to Draw
Mythical Creatures
For The Beginner

Learn To Draw Series
Jonalyn Crisologo and John Davidson

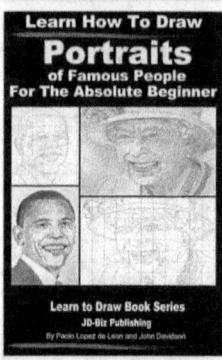

Learn How To Draw
Portraits
of Famous People
For The Absolute Beginner

Learn to Draw Book Series
JD-Biz Publishing
By Paolo Lopez de Leon and John Davidson

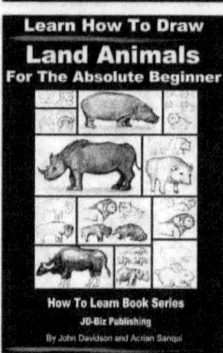

Learn How To Draw
Land Animals
For The Absolute Beginner

How To Learn Book Series
JD-Biz Publishing
By John Davidson and Adrian Sanqui

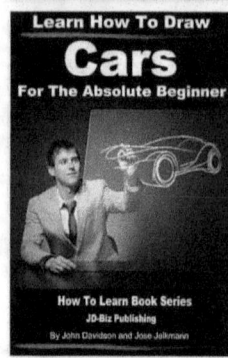

Learn How To Draw
Cars
For The Absolute Beginner

How To Learn Book Series
JD-Biz Publishing
By John Davidson and Jose Jelkmann

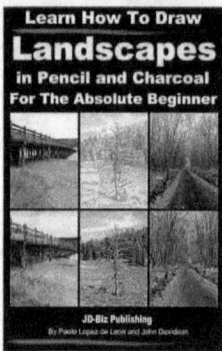

Learn How To Draw
Landscapes
in Pencil and Charcoal
For The Absolute Beginner

JD-Biz Publishing
By Paolo Lopez de Leon and John Davidson

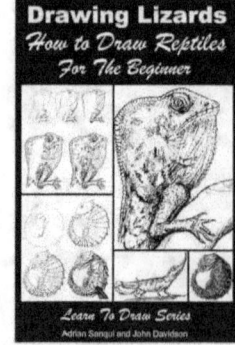

Drawing Lizards
How to Draw Reptiles
For The Beginner

Learn To Draw Series
Adrian Sanqui and John Davidson

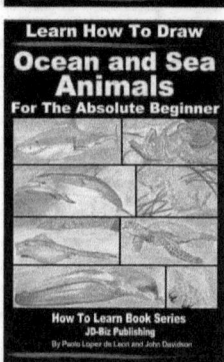

Learn How To Draw
Ocean and Sea
Animals
For The Absolute Beginner

How To Learn Book Series
JD-Biz Publishing
By Paolo Lopez de Leon and John Davidson

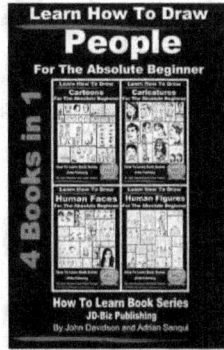

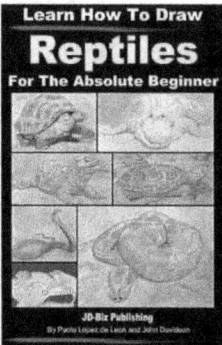

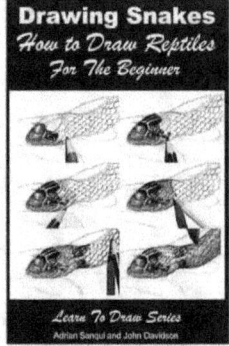

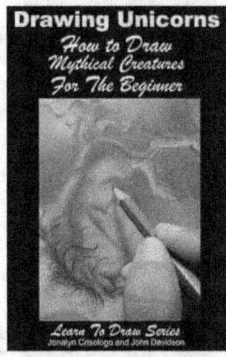

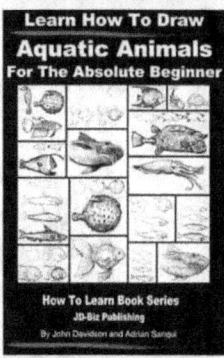

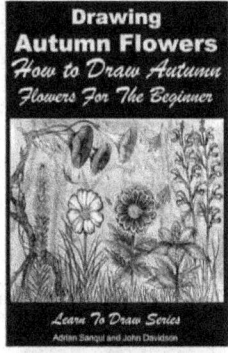

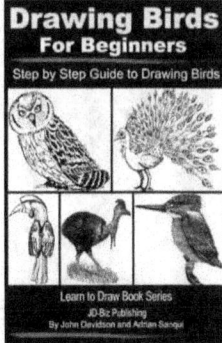

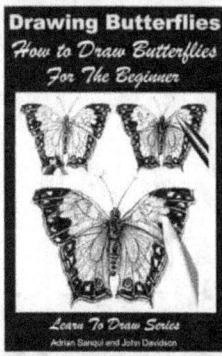

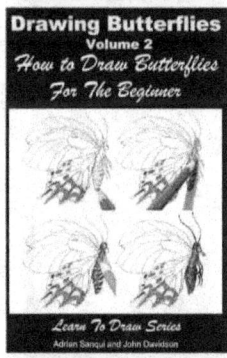

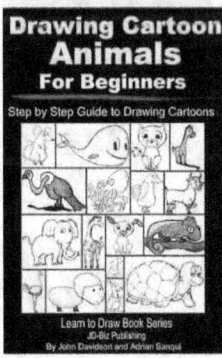

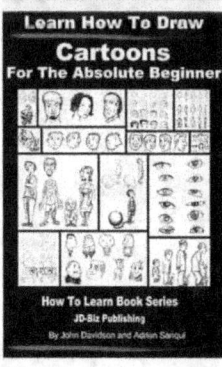

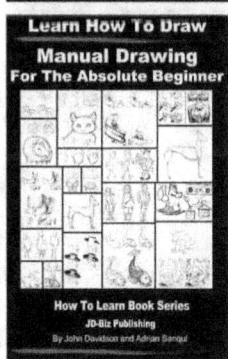

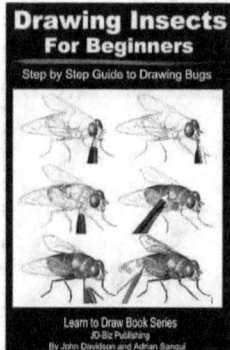

Drawing Insects
For Beginners
Step by Step Guide to Drawing Bugs

Learn to Draw Book Series
JD-Biz Publishing
By John Davidson and Adrian Sanqui

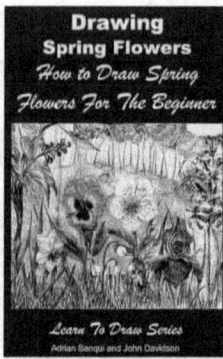

Drawing
Spring Flowers
How to Draw Spring
Flowers For The Beginner

Learn To Draw Series
Adrian Sanqui and John Davidson

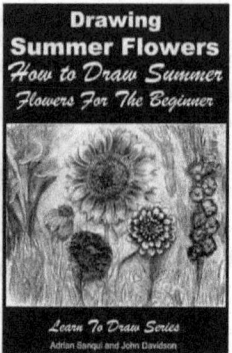

Drawing
Summer Flowers
How to Draw Summer
Flowers For The Beginner

Learn To Draw Series
Adrian Sanqui and John Davidson

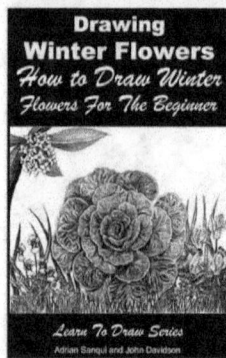

Drawing
Winter Flowers
How to Draw Winter
Flowers For The Beginner

Learn To Draw Series
Adrian Sanqui and John Davidson

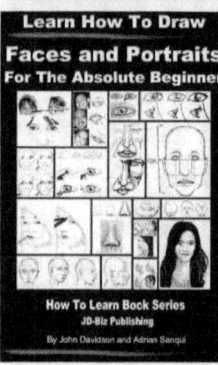

Learn How To Draw
Faces and Portraits
For The Absolute Beginner

How To Learn Book Series
JD-Biz Publishing
By John Davidson and Adrian Sanqui

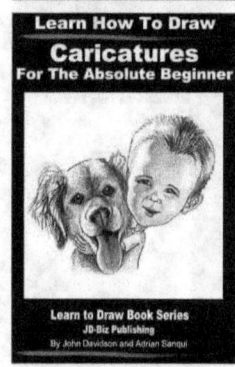

Learn How To Draw
Caricatures
For The Absolute Beginner

Learn to Draw Book Series
JD-Biz Publishing
By John Davidson and Adrian Sanqui

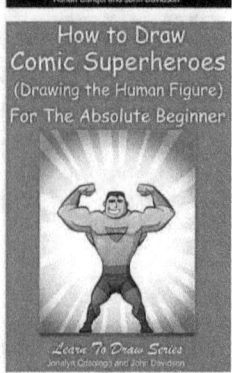

How to Draw
Comic Superheroes
(Drawing the Human Figure)
For The Absolute Beginner

Learn To Draw Series
Jonalyn Crisologo and John Davidson

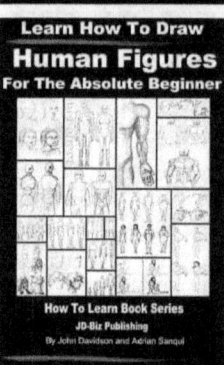

Learn How To Draw
Human Figures
For The Absolute Beginner

How To Learn Book Series
JD-Biz Publishing
By John Davidson and Adrian Sanqui

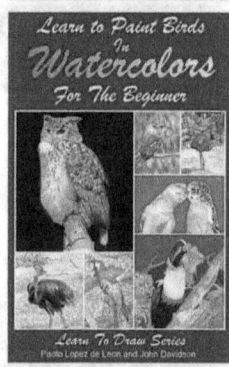

Learn to Paint Birds
In
Watercolors
For The Beginner

Learn To Draw Series
Paolo Lopez de Leon and John Davidson

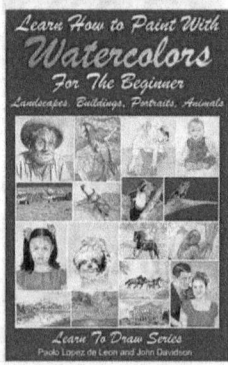

Learn How to Paint With
Watercolors
For The Beginner
Landscapes, Buildings, Portraits, Animals

Learn To Draw Series
Paolo Lopez de Leon and John Davidson

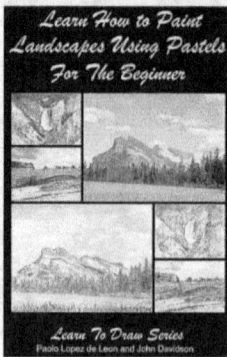

Learn How to Paint
Landscapes Using Pastels
For The Beginner

Learn To Draw Series
Paolo Lopez de Leon and John Davidson

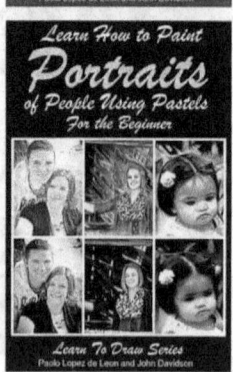

Learn How to Paint
Portraits
of People Using Pastels
For the Beginner

Learn To Draw Series
Paolo Lopez de Leon and John Davidson

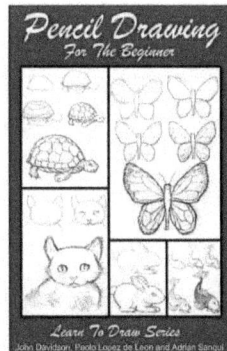

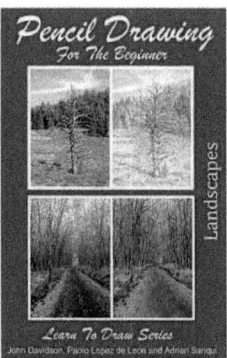

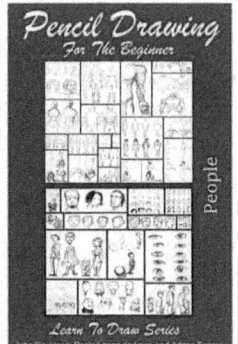

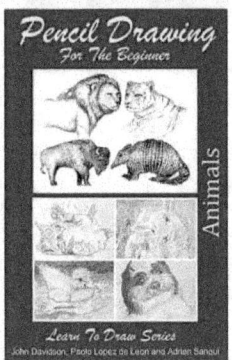

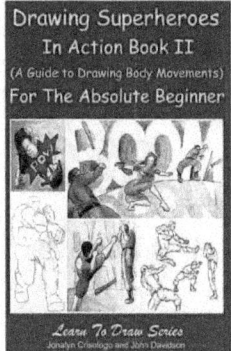

Publisher

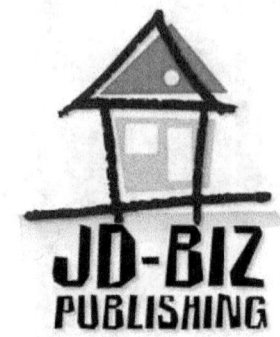

JD-Biz Corp

P O Box 374

Mendon, Utah 84325

http://www.jd-biz.com/

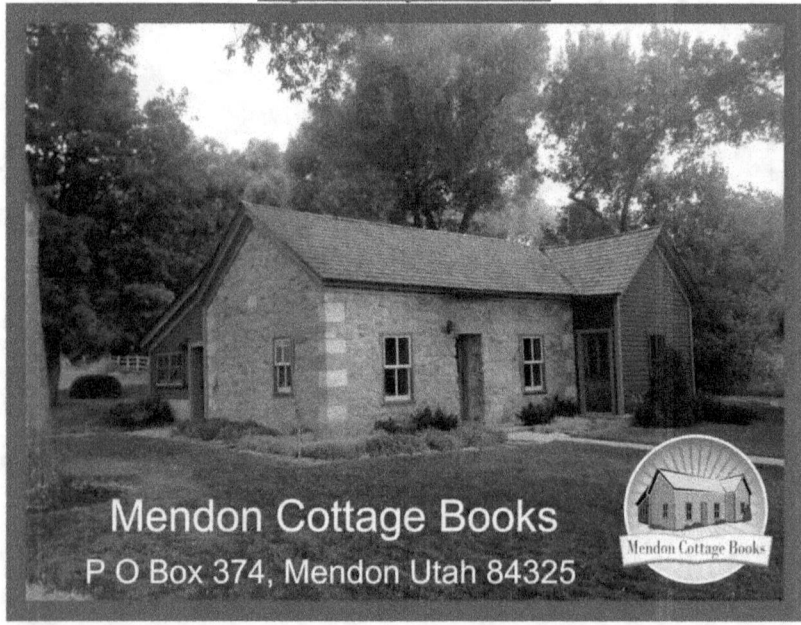